THE ART OF WRITING

by F. M. Salter

Edited by H. V. WEEKES
University of Saskatchewan
Saskatoon

REGENT COLLEGE PUBLISHING
Vancouver, British Columbia

First published by the Friends of the University of Alberta in 1967 as *The Way of the Makers.* Revised 1971 and published by Ryerson Press

This edition published 2004 by Regent College Publishing
5800 University Boulevard, Vancouver, B C. V6T 2E4 Canada
www.regentpublishing com

A catalogue record for this publication is available from the National Library of Canada

ISBN 1-57383-292-8

By the Same Author:

BOOKS

Chester Play Studies—W. W. Greg and F. M. Salter; Malone Society Publications, 1935

Bibliotheca Historica of Diodorus Siculus, translated by John Skelton—Now first edited by F. M. Salter and H. L. R. Edwards; Early English Text Society, Oxford University Press, 1956-57

Mediaeval Drama in Chester—Alexander Lectures, 1954; University of Toronto Press, 1955

ARTICLES

"Skelton's *Speculum Principis*"—*SPECULUM*, a Journal of Mediaeval Studies; Cambridge, Mass., Vol. IX, No. 1, January, 1934

"The Banns of the Chester Plays"—*Review of English Studies*, Vol. XVI, No. 62; April, 1940

"John Skelton's Contribution to the English Language," *Transactions of the Royal Society of Canada;* Third Series, Section II, Vol. XXXIX, 1945

"The Play within the Play of *First Henry IV*," *Transactions of the Royal Society of Canada*, Third Series, Section II, Vol. XL, 1946

"Shakespeare's Interpretation of *Hamlet*," *Transactions of the Royal Society of Canada*, Third Series, Section II, Vol. XLII, May, 1948

"The Problem of *King John*," *Transactions of the Royal Society of Canada*, Third Series, Section II, Vol. XLIII, June, 1949

"Shakespeare's Use of Silence," *Transactions of the Royal Society of Canada*, Third Series, Section II, Vol. XLV, June, 1951

"The Tragic Figure of the Wyf of Bath," *Transactions of the Royal Society of Canada*, Third Series, Section II, Vol. XLVIII, June 1954

"And God said, Let there be light," *Transactions of the Royal Society of Canada*, Third Series, Section II, Vol. LII, June, 1958

FOREWORD by Walter H. Johns

This work is a labor of love in two respects. The original author, the late Professor F. M. Salter, produced a number of scholarly works in his special fields of Elizabethan and Medieval literature, but he was above all a teacher, and *The Art of Writing* represents the essence of a course in creative writing, English 65, which he conducted at the University of Alberta over many years.

The original text was comprehensive and even discursive. Had Professor Salter lived longer, he would undoubtedly have reduced the size of his manuscript to the point where it could serve as a manual for students of future generations. Since his untimely death made this impossible, the difficult task of abridgment was undertaken by Dr. H. V. Weekes, himself a teacher of creative writing at the University of Saskatchewan, and a former student of Professor Salter's. He deserves our gratitude, not only for his editorial efforts, and for producing the typescript from which the present edition was made, but for his indefatigable efforts to ensure the production of the work as it stands today. In this latter respect he was ably assisted by another former student in English 65, Mr. Robert Blackburn, Librarian of the University of Toronto.

While *The Art of Writing* is not a perfect text, either in form or in substance, its virtues are best revealed in the oral delivery of the classroom rather than on the printed page. The editor has steered with skill between the Scylla of adherence to an incomplete manuscript, and the Charybdis of a completely new text which would have failed to reflect the biases and enthusiasms of the author. In this effort he has succeeded admirably and deserves our thanks.

We hope this book will provide valuable guidance and help to many generations of writers and critics in the years to come.

Walter H. Johns,
President,
University of Alberta

FOREWORD by Robert H. Blackburn

When Professor F. M. Salter met his first class of students in the "writing" course at the University of Alberta, in the autumn of 1939, he began by saying that there was only one good textbook on the subject. He paused as we sat ready to jot down the reference, and then went on to say that the book was one which he was about to write. Here is the book, revised in manuscript many times by him during his lifetime and now, finally prepared for publication by a member of the class of 1946. As I read its chapters, I hear Professor Salter speaking as he used to do.

In the classroom he read to us from our own work or from other sources either good or bad, and through comparison and example he passed on to us his love of the right word and accurate detail, his ear for apt expression, his impatience with anything shoddy. He used to say that our University on the northern frontier was the last which could enroll some students who had never before seen electric lights; he knew that most of us had never seen palaces or pirates or skylarks or maple trees or many other exotic things we had read about, and he taught us that the most important things to wonder at and write about were those within our own experience.

He assigned no topics, but required each of us to write something every week. He handed our papers back promptly, marked in red with a fine nib, and some of our pages returned more red than black. His annotations could be stern but never unkind or discouraging, and sometimes ended with an invitation to go to his office for a talk; altogether we took much more than a reasonable share of one man's time. In our excitement as "makers" many of us wrote far more than was required, went on writing even after the course was ended, and years later continued to fill the Salter mailbox with our manuscripts and our hopes.

Several members of his family of former students have become names in Canadian literature, and he used to speak of their books with a mixture of fatherly pride and professorial reservation. Others of us have lapsed into writing annual reports rather than sonnets. All of us must be grateful to F. M. Salter for a quickening of our senses, a gift we may now hope to share in some measure with those who read this book.

Robert H. Blackburn
University of Toronto Library

> I would gladly give everything I know to the light, for the good of cunning students who prize such art more highly than silver or gold. I further admonish all who have any knowledge in these matters that they write it down. Do it truly and plainly, for the sake of those who seek and are glad to learn, to the great honor of God and your own praise. If I then set something burning and ye all add to it with skilful furthering, a blaze may in time arise therefrom which shall shine throughout the world.
>
> Albrecht Dürer (1471-1528)

PREFACE

"Look you, sir, such a one
I was this present."
Twelfth Night

This book is in some sense a personal record or biography. It distils many years of my life as a teacher. It is the precipitation of a great deal of dissatisfaction with available textbooks of writing, the residue of my own thinking, the crystallization of experience and effort. But whether the result is any better than those books with which I have been impatient remains a question. That I have labored faithfully in the vineyard and endured the heat of the day, this only I claim, and claim, perhaps, with less modesty than pride.

From the first hour of my teaching I was unable to use the old eighteenth century rationale of writing, the last remnants of which still linger in our textbooks. As no alternative rationale has been forthcoming, this makeshift had to be written to provide, if nothing else, a course of lectures. It must have been in 1925 or 1926 that in final exasperation I threw over the use of textbooks altogether. Since that time, what is represented in *The Art of Writing* has been pieced together little by little. The time came when my mind seemed full of contradictory notions, when what I had learned about the art of writing was never clearly present in my thinking as a complete whole, but came forth from the disordered deep piecemeal, and only in response to the need of criticizing this or that quality in the work of a student; and it was with some grudging and weariness that I set about reducing chaos to order. It is reassuring that I still adhere to the Table of Contents which was finally straightened out in 1935. Many minor matters have altered themselves in my thinking since that time, but surely a system which has withstood the wear of so many years of teaching must have some virtue in it.

If the lines of my life fall as pleasantly in one respect during the remaining years as in the last fifteen, there will be, to answer the challenge and meet the enthusiasm of excellent students, a reason enough for these chapters—enough and to spare. They are simple and natural and friendly, these students; the ends they pursue are never silly or chimerical; they come to us to learn, and they do learn. To such students one's indebtedness grows weightier year by year, and it is in recognition of a deep obligation that in humility and love, and genuine respect, I have dedicated this book to some of them, to the little annual group of writers in English 65.

Should I have called these beginners, "writers"? Before I can adjust the focus of my spectacles, they are out in the world, editing newspapers and magazines, comminatory in pulpits, persuasive in law courts, kindly in classrooms, entertaining on the air, or publishing poetry and plays and novels, and have left me far behind, among the students of today who will join their elders tomorrow. Writers they are, then, now—or, alas, have been—or soon will be.

The varying ages and depths of these chapters will be evident to keen analysis. No doubt there are other faults. In apology, I shall say only that my proper duties have never been light, and that I have never had any lengthy period of time that might be given exclusively to such a task as this. But if, nevertheless, I really have blazed a new path toward excellence in writing, though on that point my mind is heavy and weary with doubt, others will be able to make the path easy and straight.

With so much apology and no more I draw the slip-cord and unveil the work. I hope it will withstand wind and weather for long enough to be useful.

F. M. S.—September, 1961

With *The Art of Writing* nearing publication, and with only the final editing yet to be done, Dr. F. M. Salter died late in August of 1962. In 1965, some of the graduates of English 65 resolved to lend a hand to complete the project. Practical considerations in the editing of the manuscript dictated the omission of some quoted examples, and some strictly academic and theoretical argument has been cut, but the voice speaking in the following pages is the voice of F. M. Salter, the voice that so many of us heard in the years of English 65, the voice we still can hear questioning, challenging, explaining, above all encouraging us to put forth our most honest efforts that we might reach his own shining goal—integrity and ultimate excellence in writing. To those students who have come too late to hear that voice, may *The Art of Writing* speak out strongly in his stead.

I should like to express my own thanks to all those who have contributed to the editing, proof-reading, and detail of publication, and especially to Miss Francess Halpenny, who as Managing Editor of the University of Toronto Press suggested this form of publication, and added most practical advice to assure the completion of the project.

H. V. W.—July, 1967

TABLE OF CONTENTS

Introduction

> In nature's infinite book of secrecy,
> A little I can read.
>
> *Antony and Cleopatra*

The notion that literary or artistic works are conceived in divine rage has always been enthusiastically seconded by such authors as find it flattering to be considered different from or superior to their poor earth-bound companions; but it is revealing indeed to examine variant versions of the works of great writers. Keats could be called an inspired poet if there ever was one, but Ridley's *Keats's Craftsmanship*, which shows from surviving manuscripts the stages in which such poems as "The Eve of St. Agnes" painfully crawled toward perfection, will speedily disabuse our minds. Nay, the Scriptures themselves, at least in the English version, stumbled through translation after translation toward the simplicity and majesty of the King James triumph.

There are two chief difficulties with inspiration. The first is that of establishing regular contact with the source, especially for those who write for a living. The second is the inequality that one finds in the works said to be inspired. Inspired work, assuming the source to be divine, must be work that God wants done; is not the implication of inequality sacrilegious? If the source is not divine, how can one be sure of its constant benevolence? May it not deceive with golden hopes and in the end destroy? A theory which nullifies and stultifies effort, and whose oftenest claimed products are overwhelmingly sentimental, cannot be valid. In short, the writer must determine to advance by effort and by reason, and by these alone. The best method is that of the Romans—*Nulla dies sine linea*—constant practice.

And practice, if it be practice, will certainly make perfect—but a dogged, dreary going-through-the-motions cannot be called real practice. Practice implies enthusiasm and self-criticism; it involves genuine effort and intelligence; it implies searching study of works of others. Many successful authors, like Alexander Pope, R. L. Stevenson, and Arnold Bennett, were in no way exceptionally gifted, and their struggles were painful. Pope, it is true, tells us that always he "lisped in numbers, for the numbers came," but it was not so easy as all that. Variant versions of his mature works belie him, and no man has seen his infant numbers. He was most careful to destroy them. All that his statement really means is that he served a long apprenticeship, and then, think of the physical pain and misery, the life-long migraine that wracked him, and ask if it was not labor rather than inspiration that brought his brilliant success. Stevenson and Bennett are honest enough to tell us of their miserable first efforts and how hard it was to learn; and we are told that Kipling re-wrote *Kim* nine times. Shakespeare appeared to sing so effortlessly, but can we be unaware that his work was improving in play after play from the crude *Titus Andronicus* to the masterful *Macbeth*? To permit improvement in, and with practice, the theory of Inspiration would needs contradict itself.

We need a little more faith in human reason. It is said that no cipher or cryptogram was ever devised that could not be solved. Linguists have reconstructed whole languages by means of translations or parallel passages. And in this age when the minds of men penetrate ever further into the secrets of the physical universe, shall we say that any work merely human lies beyond the power of mind to unravel? Any art can be learned, and it can be taught—the art of writing not less than other arts. In the workshop of Professor Baker of Harvard and Yale, many of the finest modern American dramatists and the best drama critics learned their skill. Behind every Caruso there is sure to be a singing teacher, behind every "hulking Tom" Guido, a Lippo Lippi.

A further consequence of the Inspiration theory is the name now given to writing in many textbooks, especially those used in secondary schools: "self-expression." If writing consisted in self-expression, most of our pupils would be defeated at once—what selves have they to express? They hardly exist as individuals. How early comes maturity, that depth and richness of character that may be worth the exhibiting to the world? Is it an accident that the best portrait of the world's best painters present *old* men and women? And even college students have barely begun to develop self-hood. The teacher's job is not to pander to self-expression, which would make instruction but a vanity indeed, but to aid students in self-creation. Every really wise teacher sees, in what his students are, a stepping stone to what they might become; for the attainment of that *becoming* no discipline is so helpful as that of writing.

If we reject self-expression as the end or aim of writing, then we destroy at once the apology given for a great deal of bad poetry. Bad poets deprecate criticism on the ground that they are expressing themselves, and that their selves are in some mystic or mysterious manner beyond the chill grasp of criticism. If so, why do they publish, why do they expect others to buy and read—as they certainly do? Witness their perennial complaint that the public will not support poets. To demand an audience for self-expression is to ask that people eavesdrop while we talk to ourselves.

"Self-expression," in short, is moonshine. But we may have something other than ourselves that is worth expressing. The very smallest child may have something to *say*, may have ideas to communicate to others, and if so he can learn to write. The pages of our literary history are glorious with the achievements of poets and prose writers in their 'teens. I take it that the true function of writing, and of all the arts, is the communication of meaning. I take it that a true writer is the arch-enemy of Babel, and that it is the function of all teachers and critics to assist him in his age-long task. It is the writers of this world upon whom we must depend to bring us all near a true federation of man—and, considering perils and the size of their task, the Antaean and Protean qualities of their opponents, and though it may not seem so, they have already gone far in this direction. It is no idle boast of Shelley's that "poets are the unacknowledged legislators of the world." They are. They are the leaveners of the lump, the quickening conscience of mankind. Further, and to more immediate point, if writing consists in the intelligible expression of meaning, teaching becomes sensible and profitable, for it will be reasonable to look for the best means of communicating any given idea. And if that is so, students will need the instruction of those who before their time have studied the art of writing.

In the pages which follow, a great deal will be found that is in some way adapted from those who in the past have written about theses of writing. There is a great deal also for which I am indebted even more to generation after generation of excellent students. The result will be like the formula for bridal wear: "Something old, something new, something borrowed, something blue." At any rate, here is a new rationale of writing. It is dependent, to state the issue yet again, upon the definition of writing as an attempt to communicate meaning; and it tries to learn the tricks and strategems of the art by means of examining the work of writers of all levels of attainment. There are many levels of writing, from craftsmanship to artistry, and it must so be recognized. This book tries also to bridge the fearful chasm which separates authors from their critics, but especially to close up that which divides teaching and practice. Whether it does these things with any success, I cannot say; but of one thing I am certain, that a new spirit and a new approach are necessary, and that surely it cannot be wrong to follow the way of the makers of literary works themselves. This, indeed, was the method of Aristotle, to look at the achievements of authorship first, and to derive principles as a result of the examination. It is when we forget the expanding area of art, and exalt tentative observations into fixed and unalterable and cramping law, that we drive a wedge between criticism and practice, between practice and instruction. As long as art exists, men will continually discover new techniques, new fields, and expanding principles, and teaching should be adaptable to what has gone before, directive to the future. Upon the rock of that belief, this book is built. It is, with me, an old rock upon which I have stood through long years of wind and weather.

F. M. S.

Part I The Craft of Writing

"What should we say, my lord?"
"Why, anything—but to th' purpose."

Hamlet

Writing may be defined as the communication of meaning through graphic symbols; a finished piece represents the ordered flow of the thought from a beginning to an end. Even bad writing is not without limit; it must start somewhere, and it cannot go on forever.

The nearest kinsman of writing among other arts is music, which also flows as a stream of sound or melody.

In writing, as in music, there must also be design. In this sense, writing may be conceived as architectural; good writing is unlikely to be done by the brick layer's method of adding brick to brick. The essential conception that one ought to hold in mind is that of a stream of thought or ideas, flowing through a piece of writing from beginning to end. There must be both direction and purpose.

Like a seismograph, then, which charts the tremors of the earth, writing records the flow of thought. There is this difference: we may take the completed record of writing and think back over it, cut out unimportant movements, straighten needless kinks, fill in gaps which in the first operation the mind has leaped across, improve the design, and render the whole more significant. For, once written, the thought becomes, as it were, frozen or molded to its form; and, like a sculptor, we may chip away and alter at will, or sandpaper and polish. Or we may scrap the whole thing and start over. It may be disheartening to write and scrap, but every successful writer has had to do it and try again, over and over. It can be a most valuable experience, for if the chart of our mental activities shows that we habitually maunder, instead of "thinking straight", if it shows that we tend to become bogged down and befuddled, we shall have learned one of the most important of all lessons, that we can only cultivate the art of writing by cultivating at the same time the art of thinking.

If all writing represents the flow of thought through concept after concept, we must, as a fundamental necessity, be precise and sure regarding the concepts themselves, and the range of their possible meanings. We must also be aware of their associations. When we use a word inexactly, we at once defeat the purpose of communication, for there can be no intelligence between persons who attach different meanings to the same words. For the purposes of mere self-expression it would, perhaps, not matter what words one used, or how one were to use them, but if we wish to convey meaning to others, we must speak in language which they also understand.

Our definition of writing may be false. If it is, I have nothing more to say; "Turne over the leaf, and chese another tale." But if it is true, and writing does consist in the communication of meaning, we must ask: Has the thought value? Is it important? Is it worth the number of words used to express it? Is it worth the time required to read it? The writer must first of all be sure he has something to say, and that what he has to say is worth saying. For the first test of literary value, and the final test, will always be Significance.*

* Be careful, now; do not allow me to mislead you, or lead you into a trap. This entire book stands on that statement, and we had better be sure of it. Here is a test: why has such a poem as "Jabberwocky" enduring value? On the surface, it is pure nonsense. Can nonsense be significant?

A. MATERIALS AND AIDS

"Take twelve eggs . . ."
Mrs. Beaton's Cook Book

If significance is necessary in writing, so is knowledge to the writer. Out of ignorance nothing of even ephemeral significance can be written. The writer needs the broadest possible education and understanding of the world. How can a man interpret the present if he knows nothing of the past? How can a man know his own country if he cannot compare it with other countries and peoples? Even for the work of the local newspaper, a reporter must have some "background": if an Einstein comes to town, we cannot begin to interview him without some knowledge of science and its methods; to interview a statesman even a cub reporter must have some glimmering of international affairs. Or shall we be reduced, when the golden opportunity arrives, to telling the world what these great men ate for breakfast? The real writers of the world are necessarily men of enquiring mind; they do not count lost the days and years devoted to becoming knowledgeable.

There are three sources of materials and ideas for writing:—books, conversation, and direct observation of life.

Chaucer remarked centuries ago:

> For out of olde feldes, as men seith,
> Cometh al this newe corn fro yere to yere;
> And out of olde bokes, in good feith,
> Cometh al this newe science that men lere.

The statement is true enough, but it goes too far. Chaucer himself, at a later time, demonstrated how much new science or knowledge he could gain from direct observation of life. Nevertheless, the greatest single source of material for writers will be books—if they are properly read.

The proviso is important. The only kind of reading likely to be starting ideas buzzing in the mind is critical reading, reading that challenges every statement, weighs every chapter, notes the technique of the author, sees through every artifice, and realizes the full import of every sentence and fact. One must read with the mind awake, not heavy or drowsy. Many people read to put themselves to sleep at night. Such reading, which is not an intellectual activity at all is not going to inspire new ideas or add to one's knowledge. Many people read a novel for the story alone, and miss the author's interpretation of life, his artistry, his philosophy. Nobody ever learned anything from that kind of reading. It may be restful, but it will not stimulate; for real exercise we do not stroll or loiter, but stride.

Nor can there be any objection to reading for a more active and keener enjoyment, reading that offers an "escape" from the tedious or the humdrum, when we uncritically surrender to "magic casements opening on the foam of perilous seas, in faery lands forlorn," or we thrill to adventure or the life of other men or of other lands. And we may read for information, paying no attention to the *how* since it is the *what* we want. But to learn to write we must learn to read expertly. And we must also realize that all of us are deeply influenced by our environments, by the food we eat, the friends we choose, and the homes we live in; that whatever casual acquaintance we may have among those who have written before us, we must give the depths and sincerities of friendship only to those writers who have dignified their calling.

The term "book" in this connection ought to apply to all records of intellectual activity. A visit to an art gallery ought as much as a good book to send us home with treasure trove. So should attendance at public lectures, theatres, concerts, motion pictures, and visits to public monuments. Nor is it even necessary that the book be good if we are intent upon learning; the "horrible example" has as much to teach us as a piece of adequate craftsmanship; and though the lesson is taught in reverse, it may be all the more memorable for its shocking demonstration of the faults into which we might fall. If the term "book" is used in this broad sense, to include every form of art, every record of the intellect at work, then Chaucer's remark rounds out toward full truth—but the "newe science" is only to be found by minds that seize upon details and broad truths alike, and carry every thesis further to apply it more widely or differently, and simplify complexities, always keenly pursuing new ideas.

This seeking of stimulation of one's intellectual life from books is a very different thing from plagiarism, which is simple dishonesty. We cannot take too great pains to make sure that our work is entirely our own; if there is the slightest indebtedness, an acknowledgement is required. Acknowledgement is always graceful, is always honest. It is like a note for money borrowed. But if after reading a book on the evolution of man, one should distort the theory into a fanciful paper on the evolution of shoe-laces or drinking-cups, there is obviously no debt and no acknowledgement to make.

The key to good reading, then, is attentiveness and interest. And these are not gifts with which some persons are born and which others may never hope to enjoy; they are the result of cultivation and habit, and they are worth cultivation. Without interest in his work, nobody can hope for success. The writer must be alive not only to human beings, but to everything that touches on the art of writing, and especially to books which are themselves not only records of human life but models from which he learns his craft.

The second source of material is conversation. It is often lamented that conversation is a lost art in the modern world. It has never been anything but a lost art since the days when Adam and Eve exclaimed together about their strange new world. To every Adam and every Eve since then, the world has been, at least during some moments of vision, new and strange; and it would be astonishing if modern men and women were completely tongue-tied. But many of the lost arts advance just twenty years behind the date from century to century.

The fact is that anybody who wants to talk will find many a rapier wit ready for a duel, from that of the delivery boy who loiters on the back stoop to that of the judge who lingers toward the bench. And the same key, that unlocks the treasure house of writing, opens the door to all sorts of provocative and sustained conversations: the key of interest. Chance-met travellers will enter upon whole Iliads and Odysseys of biography, complete if not with catalogues of ships, at least with intricate family trees; and a little interest is the open sesame to whole worlds of entertainments of the most bracing kind: fact, liberally spiked with fiction. Catch people at leisure, let them learn that you have ears to hear, and see that there are fascinating talkers in the world—farmers, mechanics, and craftsmen, housewives, professionals—all waiting to unbosom themselves of the very stuff of literature. Those who say that the art of conversation is lost, confess that they don't know where or how to find what any stranger can charm out of the air all around them. The art of conversation belongs in some degree to every person breathing, and the fairy wand that gives speech to frozen statues is interest.

The third source of material for the writer is his own fresh observation of life and the world. Interest, again, unlocks the hoard, sharpening our senses and stimulating our awareness of all that goes on around us. It can fill our days with wonder and bring us home in the evening freighted with material for writing. It will not be a question of searching for something to write, but of selecting from rich stores, but unless we can soak up materials at every pore, the kingdom of active writers will be closed to us. The desire may abide with us, but it is surely the most obvious of all things that if we have nothing to say, we can say nothing.

These: books, conversation, and the world about us, are the real sources of material. What sorts of things should we select? The one writes what he knows the world wants; the second writes what he thinks the world might want; the third writes what he himself wants to write. The first is the purveyor of cheap and shoddy goods, even when he has chosen as his subject matter piety and virtue, as sometimes he has; the second is possibly a good writer on the wrong track; the third is the artist. In him burns the true light. He does not care whether he has an audience or not; he writes what he must write, the thing in which he is interested. Only when it is written does he seek the market place. If a man is really interested in what he has to say, then he cannot fail sooner or later to find an audience, and sometimes the largest of all audiences.

If a man really means it, the world is obliged to listen; it cannot refrain from listening. That is why enthusiasm is set down in this book as one of the few available criteria for the judgment of a piece of artistic work. The great writer is he who "holdeth children from play, and old men from the chimney corner." The great writer is the ancient mariner who holds the wedding guest by the sheer power of a tale that *must* be told. The great writer is the man who means it! He can only mean what he is interested in saying. Any other enthusiasm is necessarily false and rings hollow.

Anyone who intends to learn to write will do best to aim high, and to follow the methods and the technique of those who have written best. And those who in all generations have written best are the ones who might say with Mark Antony, but quite simply: "Here I am to say what I do *know*."

Like every other workman, the writer needs tools and equipment. First of all, a dictionary. The greatest monument of the English-speaking peoples is the *Oxford English Dictionary* (OED), also known as the *New English Dictionary* (NED), and as the *Murray Dictionary* in honor of the distinguished first editor. OED is built on historical principles. That is to say, it tries to follow every word from its first introduction into English down to the present time, and to give a complete account of all the changes of meaning through which a word has moved. Herein lies the importance of OED to writers, to whom it is always important to know not only what words do mean, but what in the past they did mean. Otherwise, one might well use words with no sense of their flavor, or of the aura that clings to them from former associations. OED, in short, shows us the pedigree and life history of words and helps us to understand both their denotations and their connotations. If we understand a man better by knowing some of the experiences of his childhood, so we know words better because we know their histories.

A work similar to the OED, and inaugurated under the direction of its last editor, is the *Dictionary of American Speech*, in four folio volumes, completed in 1944 at the University of Chicago.

Next in value to the OED is the *Webster International*. It is an extremely efficient work, and makes itself a general reference work as well as a dictionary. One useful feature of it is the lists which it gives of synonyms of any word that lends itself to such treatment, with discussions which show exact shades of meaning involved and the specific uses of each synonym.

Probably the most convenient dictionary for young students is the *Webster Collegiate*, a very handy desk volume. The one-volume *Oxford* is also useful, and Funk and Wagnalls *Standard College Dictionary* is in its Canadian edition a remarkable source of information.

An intelligent person will learn the meaning of all the symbols and abbreviations necessary for presenting vast information in a small compass, and, among other things, he will discover soon that he must know something about English grammar. The abbreviation *tr.* after a verb has meaning, but only to those who know what a transitive verb is.

There are a great number of grammar texts now available, and all cover pretty much the same material. Somewhat more advanced is the *Dictionary of Modern English Usage* by H. W. Fowler, which presumes a basic knowledge of grammar.

In addition the writer would do well to get the style book of a publishing house, the Modern Languages Association's style booklet, or *Scholarly Reporting in the Humanities*, all of which explain what a writer should know about the preparation of manuscripts.

Next in value to a good dictionary will be a good book of synonyms. Roget's *Thesaurus* is still the best known, and it is of great help, although now somewhat old-fashioned. There is now available an excellent *Dictionary of Synonyms* by Webster. Again, however, a tool is of value only if you know how to use it. Roget offers only lists of synonyms, but no two words mean exactly the same thing. We call words synonyms when they touch each other on some common ground of meaning, as, for example, *shack* and *castle*, which are synonymous in that both imply human shelter from the elements; but to use either one in place of the other indiscriminately would be ridiculous.

A further suggestion may be made regarding tools. Anyone hoping to make a living by writing, or to enjoy himself by it, ought to know how to type. He ought to learn to compose on the typewriter. For all ordinary purposes a portable is as good as an office machine, if it is not so light that one has to hitch after it all over the room, and it is easier to carry about. The reasons why a typewriter should be one of a writer's tools are several: type is colder than handwriting, and the amateur is much less likely to be enamored of his typing than he is to be incapable of altering a single glowing, hand-written word. Unless he can freely revise, it is unlikely that he will proceed very far in the art of writing. Again, typewritten paragraphs as a rule seem much briefer than the same paragraphs written with pen and ink, though not so brief as ordinary print. Many students never learn to write for this reason, never learn to give body, illustration, shape, and emphasis to their thought in well-built, rounded paragraphs. Then a third advantage of the typewriter is that it is more rapid, and so more efficient in keeping up with our ideas. When writing by hand we are often unable to "get it all down," as anyone's experience during final examinations will prove, and we leave gaps which we then fail to fill in later. Frequently the flow of writing when recorded by a tiring hand is so erratic that no amount of polishing afterwards will render it more agreeable. Finally, as a purely practical matter, one can do more work, less painfully, and more legibly, in the same time with a typewriter. Anything that reduces misery for all is a boon.

B. MECHANICS

> "Thus Gods are made,
> And whoso makes them otherwise shall die."
> Rudyard Kipling: *Evarra and his Gods*

(1) *Sentence*

The sentence is ordinarily defined as "a group of words expressing a complete thought." This definition is manifestly absurd. It may apply equally well to a paragraph, a chapter, a book. Is not a book a group of words expressing a complete thought? Wherein does it differ from a sentence? The definition does not, as a true definition should, exclude those things which are not sentences.

The worst fault of the definition is that a sentence cannot, except under very unusual circumstances, express a complete thought at all. Here are some sentences chosen at random from the stream of various writings:

> It does nothing of the sort.
> That was all the express note taken that Molly had disappeared from the eyes of men.
> I must own, that of late days, I have found this a limited source of information.

Examples might be endlessly multiplied. The fact is that if a sentence does make complete sense, aside from its context, we have either bad writing or extravagant accident. A sentence can only begin to make complete sense by itself if it uses no pronouns or other words of reference.

Pronouns bear, in themselves, little or no meaning; they are chameleon words which take color from their background, which derive meaning from their antecedents. But even when sentences lack pronoun or other word of reference, they may still lack meaning. Take "The man agreed." This is a sentence, but does it make complete sense? What did he agree to, and under what circumstances? If a sentence is torn from its context, it ought not to make complete sense; if it does the context is unnecessary and should be deleted, for it has proved to be mere wind.

This ancient, standard definition of the sentence, moreover, does not notice the most obvious of all things, punctuation upon which the sense may depend. Here are two sentences:

> The inspector says the teacher is a fool.
> The inspector, says the teacher, is a fool.

We have the same words; two commas reverse the meaning. Should, then, we say that a sentence is a group of words making complete sense when properly punctuated?

Even so, we should still find ourselves in difficulties. In *The Comedy of Errors*, Antipholus of Ephesus says to the goldsmith, "A man is well holp up that trusts to you." He means the opposite of what he says. Further, with one set of words we can express at one single time two or more separate meanings, even meanings mutually incompatible. Otherwise, what do we mean by double entendre? What do we mean by irony and allegory? When Dryden writes of a "milk-white hind"—

> Panting and pensive now she ranged alone,
> And wandered in the kingdoms, once her own,

one meaning is obvious. For the other we need a key. The allegorical meaning is: "The Roman Catholic Church [the Hind], pre-eminent in purity [milk white], was once the sole church." We must conclude that the sentence is simply a conduit through which meaning can flow, and that the thought may be separable from the words and even contradictory to them. When the words are pinned down and equally meaningful to speaker and listener, we can understand that such expressions as "Look what the cat dragged in!" or "You old horse!" may breathe the warmth of purest love.

If the usual definition of sentence must be discarded as useless, the usual division of sentence into subject and predicate may be kept with a proviso: any unit, whether sentence, paragraph, chapter, essay, short story, poem, biography, or book must have a subject. And any complete piece of writing must say something about its subject—that is, must have a predicate. In so far as a sentence bears upon the meaning of the paragraph in which it appears, it must concern itself with the subject of that paragraph, and similarly with the subject of the essay, chapter, or longer work from which the paragraph is taken. For example, we may isolate the sentence, "The rain falls upon the just and the unjust," from its context.

The subject is rain. But the sentence, let us say, is taken from a paragraph which shows Nature is impartial. The immediate sentence, then, is read and understood by the reader as part of that paragraph, and it has an external subject, Nature. But this paragraph, let us suppose, is taken from a sermon which proves that God is love. Again we must read the sentence, "The rain falls upon the just and the unjust," in the light of the whole sermon; and it really has, therefore, one internal subject, Rain, and two external subjects, Nature and God. By itself the sentence can be necessarily only incomplete as a representation of the thought of the author because the context is missing; to make complete sense of it, we must restore whatever is lost when the context is taken away, as, "Because God is love, His servant Nature is impartial. Therefore the rain falls upon the just and the unjust." All we can say, then, is that a sentence is the smallest structural unit within which meaning can flow. It is the movement, the flow, that is significant.

(2) *Paragraph*

That the paragraph is as real an entity as the sentence there can be no reasonable doubt. It is, however, a modern invention—as every reader of the King James Bible will know. It belongs to an age when the mass of human beings was capable of understanding elements larger than the single sentence. Children used to learn to read letter by letter, spelling out words; later they read by words. To read sentence by sentence is a greater achievement, but modern educated men read paragraph by paragraph. If it is possible to do so, it follows that the paragraph must have as much entity as a letter, a word, or a sentence, and it has.

This is not to say that a paragraph is merely a collection of sentences; it is not even just a group of sentences that deal with the same topic. Rather the paragraph is the foil or setting which enhances, enlarges, deepens, or modifies the meaning of every sentence in it. Here is a sentence from the paragraph of a student: "And now the word has lost its meaning." To be perfectly fair, let us render the sentence more specific than it is in the original: "And now the word *freedom* has lost its meaning." When we supply the paragraph setting, that sentence ought to take on more meaning than it has when torn from its context. Here is the paragraph:

Political Freedom

It was once a word of shining magic. The earliest human beings blundered somehow blindly toward it. Socrates whispered it to the youth of Athens. King John unwillingly signed his name to it in the Magna Carta. A ragged mob screamed for it at the walls of the Bastille. Men bled for it on the fields of Flanders. Thousands more have died for it in the war just ended. *And now the word has lost its meaning.* It has been shouted too loud and too often by the big-mouthed, hollow-headed men who believe in nothing but the booming sound of their own voices, and who fear real political freedom as much as they fear local obscurity. The simple man listens, dulled by the noise and awed by the never-ending flow of words. He does not talk of it, but he knows, better than those who do, that only the word itself and all its glib associations are dead. The man on the brightly lit platform booms on, but he cannot see beyond the footlights. He cannot see that the echoing hall is empty. For the man who sat there quietly listening has gone out to fight not for the word but for the thing, knowing that we cannot talk convincingly about things unless we have them. Real freedom is still magic.

R. L. Gordon

Against the story of man's blundering search and struggle, does not that sentence take on more meaning than when it stands alone? If it were not so, then we should throw away either the paragraph or the sentence, for it would have been proved that one or the other is unnecessary. Test other sentences in the same way: "The man on the brightly lit platform booms on, but he cannot see beyond the footlights"; "A ragged mob screamed for it at the walls of the Bastille"; "Real freedom is still magic." Do not these sentences all mean more in context than alone? The paragraph, then, is a device which enables every sentence in it to carry more than its single, unaided weight; it is a unit of thought, and when we create a paragraph, we set the flow of meaning so in motion that the overtones and undertones carry through and around these mere units of structure that we call sentences. The paragraph is a device which makes our sentences come alive and carry an overplus of meaning. It compels them to co-operate in the achievement of a total meaning or effect greater than their sum.

But let us remember that the paragraph also may be a unit in a still greater structure, and itself gain meaning by its context. And let us remember that, like any other unit of writing, it should have a subject and a predicate. Properly written, a paragraph is simply a sentence raised to the second power. It is a sentence, expanded, and heightened to render it more significant. The square of four is sixteen; a paragraph is similarly a square of the essential sentence out of which it takes its being. Now it would be absurd, of course, to insist upon exact mathematical multiplication. Two different writers might square the same basic sentence with very different results. But it seems true that if a sentence represents the first stage of thought consisting, as it were, in the multiplication of two or more concepts then the paragraph must represent the second stage of thought and so will have just as much entity as a sentence has—and more.

Sentences are classified, according to structure, as simple, compound, and complex; rhetorically, they are classified as imperative, declarative, interrogative, and exclamatory; in method or style, we call them loose, periodic, and balanced. We might, if we desired do the same thing with paragraphs and even larger elements of writing, although, with the expansion of sentences into paragraphs, the distinctions are naturally blurred. Books, essays, and paragraphs all tend to become declarative; but the letter of any schoolgirl to her friend will supply exclamatory paragraphs—and, at a somewhat higher level, they will be found everywhere in the work of Thomas Carlyle. For imperative paragraphs, check the orders of any general, or look at any code of laws. Nor would interrogative paragraphs be hard to find, paragraphs which ask a question; they come most frequently at the beginning of articles, presenting a problem which the article may solve. Compound paragraphs are common. A paragraph expanding the sentence, "Jennie was drowning, and Frank ran to the rescue," might well be compound; or, if it stressed one clausal idea more than the other, it could turn complex. Lincoln's Gettysburg address is a good example of a complex declarative paragraph. Boiled down, it says: "Political liberty, for which many Americans have died, must not be allowed to perish." But it renders this sentence, which does not appear in it, more significant, raising it to the second power.

Let it not be thought that "topic sentences" are here under discussion. Topic sentence technique can result in nothing but wooden and mechanical writing. The very idea of a topic sentence, the sentence which gives the substance of the paragraph in brief, overlooks the necessity of predicate and point; and the fact is that topic sentences can be found in the work of no greater author—in order to create examples, the authors of textbooks trim and alter and violate their originals. They show us not what the makers of literature have done, but what they should have done—if they had been badly taught. Further, since the topic sentence inevitably gravitates toward the beginning, it cultivates textbookish writing: first the definition in blackface, then the explanation. If we understand the definition, we need not read the explanation. Textbook writing makes no attempt at suspense; and since textbooks are synonymous with dullness, it is perhaps as well that such writers as Dickens, Thackeray, Conrad, and Galsworthy wrote before the topic sentence technique was born. The sentence the square of which is the paragraph cannot, in the very nature of things, appear exactly in the paragraph at all.

It is instructive to analyse paragraphs in books and determine to what type they belong. We shall find that just as declarative sentences greatly outnumber other types in ordinary writing, so come declarative paragraphs even more frequently than other types of paragraphs. It is equally instructive to write paragraphs of various sorts, just to get the feel of the paragraph as a thought unit, and to prove that the basic idea does acquire greater meaning, a greater impressiveness, greater piquancy or flavor from the working.

Several tests of the value of paragraphs, one's own or those of others, spring from this discussion: Does the paragraph have a subject? Has it a predicate or point? Does it lend to every sentence in it greater prestige or significance than the same sentence would have if it stood alone? Is the logic clear, and does the thought develop? Does the whole thing land on its feet? Does the thought move forward and reach an objective? Is the idea sufficiently enhanced by the paragraph to justify the number of words expended?

While studying paragraphs, we should note average lengths. Pick out a medium paragraph from a book and copy it by hand, and be amazed at its length. The size will of course vary with the material. Most narrative paragraphs will be found to be about seventy-five words, in contrast to descriptive ones which average more than two hundred, and expository ones, which may average over three hundred. That is, the more involved and complicated the thought, the more room will be necessary to express it.

(3) *Larger Units*

Just as the sentence forms a structural unit within the paragraph, so the paragraph may be a larger structural unit within longer works. And just as the sentence gains an overplus of meaning from its context, so may the paragraph. We must be chary of saying that even the paragraph must "make complete sense." And in the same way a paragraph may be considered as a sentence raised to the second power, so a chapter may be treated as a sentence raised to the third power. Now there are, of course, certain differences between story and essay and between drama and fiction, but all forms of writing must exhibit some basic or essential similarity, just as all mammals do. Otherwise mammals cannot be called mammals, and writing cannot be called writing. To be accurately classified as a piece of writing at all, the piece, however long or short, must have a subject and a predicate; it must talk about something, and it must say something about that topic; it must communicate meaning. Further, the differences in literary forms go straight back to the sentences they expand, for there is as much difference between a narrative sentence and an argumentative one relatively, as there is between a short story and a legal proof.

We may even speak of poems, plays, novels, and non-fiction prose works as imperative, interrogative, exclamatory, or declarative. Thus the *Queen's Rules and Admiralty Orders* is simply an imperative book, as is any code of laws. But propaganda stories, plays, novels, and books are also imperative in that they "command, request, or plead for" certain actions or conduct in response. Many a travel book is nothing but one huge exclamation mark, and the Book of Psalms a long exclamation about the goodness of God. Frank Stockton's "The Lady or the Tiger," like Chaucer's Frankelyn's Tale and hundreds of medieval "debats," does nothing but ask a question. And what do we mean by "problem" plays and novels unless that they also present in detail a question which the audience must answer?

(4) *Planning*

Any work is the better for being planned. The writer who fails to plan will find himself in difficulties, and the exasperation and frustration involved may bring his writing career to an early end. The young writer is most likely to write his conclusions first, and then, in order to keep going at all, get off the track. Every college professor of English reads hundreds of essays every year which start out bravely and dribble off to nothing, or which present conclusions in the first few sentences and wind up miles away from the subject.

No one would think of entering upon the construction of a house or a skyscraper without a blueprint; design is a prerequisite of each monument; it is equally a prerequisite of good writing. The materials also will to some extent dictate the design. It is impossible for the builder to create a skyscraper out of wood. So it must be in writing: when the writer knows what materials to use, he will be able to draw up an intelligent plan.

Again, any competent builder can take the architect's plan and construct the building intended. There may be small differences between the work of two builders who embody in concrete and steel the project designed in the same blueprint; but practically speaking, two houses built from the same plan by different builders will be the same. We should make our writing plans in such fashion that another person could write the essay or story if we fail. As a matter of fact, even a short interruption or interval does make another person of oneself. Many a student has had an idea on Monday which he could not recapture on Friday when his theme was due. The essay we thought so clear a month ago seems strange and bewildering to us today; if we have not made the blueprint specific, we cannot write it. When even longer intervals pass, greater difficulties follow. But if the plan is specific and workmanlike, the design will still be there to make completion possible.

Further, a plan, a blueprint, a design enables us to see in our work the faults before they are committed to writing. The plan can be studied objectively and with ease. Are there flaws in the argument? Does the thought flow smoothly? Does the whole thing merit further labor? All errors may be corrected, the design made more effective, the point established more clearly, if the blueprint is made first.

Unplanned writing, as every teacher and editor in the world can testify, is a contradiction in terms; it is mere drooling.

There must be method, and good method. First gather material. It must then be arranged in a plan. Let the plan stand a while, and set yourself to other things. Attack it again, with as much detachment as possible, as if it were written by somebody else. When you are sure it is right, go ahead. Think it all through, and write as fast as it is possible to get things down on paper. Let the result stand again and grow cold. Go over it once more; correct it if necessary, ease the joints, direct the flow more smoothly or more tempestuously as it seems desirable, sharpen the expressiveness of every sentence, every paragraph. The result should be good work. If you can rewrite many times, all the better, if you don't work it to death; but rewriting once is necessary even for experienced writers. All these operations will take less time than the novice usually spends on drooling.

The more fluent writer will perhaps find that planning seems to cramp him somewhat, is more difficult than his usual flux. The coach meets this situation every day; the runner has speed, but his form is all wrong. To correct the form is to lessen the speed at first; but in the end the runner has incomparably greater ease, speed, and staying power. The boxer has a rough efficacy of his own. To correct an awkwardness of style is to destroy for a time the force of his punch, but in the end, his grace and sureness and efficiency in offence and defence are far superior to his crude early flailing and haymaking. So it will be with those writers who have learned fluency and nothing else.

I must insist on this point, for merely fluent novices prove the despair of every teacher. They *know* that writing is easy—but they know wrong. No art and no craft is easy. The best writers do "sweat blood" like Conrad, and the best books have been through the fire at least seven times.

A plan which merely lists headings is of little value. One may be able to remember for a short time what one intended to say about these subjects; but the other person whom one so speedily becomes can be unable to work up the design. Here are two plans, now somewhat of the past, which deal with the same material. Even after so many long years, one of them could still be worked up, though with a degree of trouble since the events are now forgotten; but the other was useless a day or two after it was drawn up.

Title: *F. D. Roosevelt*	Title: *Roosevelt the Great*
	Thesis: As Roosevelt seems dangerous to me, I shall not vote for him.

I. R. as a man	I. During the campaign of 1934, he made promises that he could not have hoped to fulfill.
II. R. as a President	II. He seems to have no real regard for the Constitution.
III. Infantile Paralysis	III. The only thing that I can see of value in his work is the inauguration of the N.Y.A.
IV. The present campaign	IV. Whenever a huge number of prominent members of a candidate's own party "take a walk," it is about time for the rest of the country to do the same.

In longer works, there is a further advantage in planning. The plan enables the author to write first any part he likes. If he is tired, he may choose an easy bit and leave more difficult things till the time when he feels fresher. Some parts may require careful, long research which cannot be done at the moment, and there may be many another difficulty.

It should be said, however, that the writer who waits for these right "moods" or for inspiration will probably wait forever. A right mood comes from interest and from doing things regularly at the same time and place. When the workman walks into his shop, he is ready to go to work, however he may have felt ten minutes earlier—"The labor we delight in, physics pain."

Remember, then, that finished writing is "frozen thought." There must always be one or more subjects and one or more predicates; these can be set down as the "thesis" of the projected work. In the elucidation of that thesis, various materials will be needed. And for each paragraph or section of the intended paper, a sentence can be found, which, when "squared," expanded, or rendered more significant, will become that paragraph or section. By inspecting the order of these sentences, we can see how logically the thought moves through the whole. It does not matter whether we engage in narrative, drama, poetry, or biography: the basic method is the same.

(5) *Titles*

Almost the whole art of writing is implicit in good planning. An attractive title, however, will disarm many readers and lead them to read pieces which otherwise might not appeal. Titles ought to appear at the same time as the plan or outline, and should not be left until afterward. It will often be difficult or impossible to find a good title for a finished piece of work, whereas a title chosen beforehand will be true to the central idea and will fit itself into the writing as it proceeds. With a thesis definitely in mind, the selection of a title is easier than otherwise. It is also of advantage to be able to check each part of your paper against the title; if it does not fit with the title, that part is off the topic.

In some types of writing, the title should be plain-spoken; the thesis itself, abbreviated, is proper. In newspapers, headings ought to give the pith of the story to him who runs and reads. In ordinary business affairs, allusive or artistic captions are out of place. A paper to be read before a Medical Association ought to have a title stating as nearly as possible the exact province of the material, and its specific contribution to existing knowledge; for example: "The Cause of Cancer: a Filterable Virus." Such titles prevent those who desire information from wasting time over articles which have no real interest for them.

For works intended to be recreational or artistic, an allusive title is better. Such titles should not give away the point. One of my students submitted a story called "Hail" to a magazine; it was an excellent story, but was rejected. The editor said that the end, after the storm, was anticlimactic. It was not; it seemed anticlimatic only because the title had led him to expect a hailstorm as climax. When the title was changed, there was no trouble. O. Henry was especially adept at clever titles. "The Ransom of Red Chief" in its words, its rhythm, and its alliteration has a definite appeal; and "The Gift of the Magi," "Cupid and the Archer," *The Gentle Grafter*, and *Cabbages and Kings* have equal effectiveness. His titles have also that special significance which proves that they must have been set before the stories were written, and worked themselves into the texture with peculiar aptness.

Titles should be as concise as possible; not only brief, but to the point. Alliteration sometimes adds a special grace; antithesis adds crisp effectiveness. Many excellent titles consist only of one word each: *Kidnapped*, *Macbeth*, *Youth*. A list of the best books to be found in the world would probably be a list also of the best titles: *Hamlet*, *Revolt in the Desert*, *The Seven Pillars of Wisdom*, *King Lear*, *Pride and Prejudice*, *Old Mortality*, *The Divine Comedy*, *Paradise Lost*, and so on. The same principles underlie good writing everywhere, and good titles are written by good writers.

(6) *Beginning and End*

Having planned and outlined his project, and having selected a title, the writer is ready to record it. How shall he begin? It is true, of course, the beginning will have been provided for when the plan was made, but as beginning seems to involve a sort of special mental hazard, a word or two about it will not be amiss.

The textbooks have always laid down rules which no successful authors have ever followed; and there is the age-old insistence upon Introduction, Body, and Conclusion. These have inevitably been considered three separate parts of any piece of writing; and many students confess themselves capable of embalming bodies, but quite unable to get them coffined in introduction and conclusion. Their worry is quite unnecessary. If they can set the stream of writing flowing at all, they can guide it; and a piece of writing is one thing, not three. With this statement Plato himself, from whom the threefold division ultimately derives, would agree, for what he actually said was, "There should be a middle, beginning, and end, *adapted to one another and to the whole*."

It cannot be too strenuously insisted that writing is a stream of thought, flowing from beginning to end, flowing through and around sentences, paragraphs, chapters, according to the length of the work: it is anything but a foundation, out-walls, and roof. It is best to forget that such words as Introduction, Body, and Conclusion exist.

If an introduction has any excuse for existence, it is that it limits the field of a piece of writing, indicates its interest, and tries to justify in advance the readers' expenditure of time. It is a sort of porch which invites us to enter the house—but one of the commonest faults of student essays is that the porch will be bigger than the house. For a book-length manuscript, a separate and formal introduction may be necessary, although often it is not; but in short pieces one hardly needs worry, for, as a matter of fact, it is practically impossible to write without an introduction. If one writes about a subject at all, the subject is unavoidably mentioned—that is to say, introduced. The way to start any piece of writing is to start it, get in and get going. The sooner the stream of thought begins to flow, the better. But the longer the writer stands there on the brink, trying to get his courage up to go swimming, the more it is painful to himself and to the reader.

Similarly, the way to stop writing is to stop; and the very best place to stop is at the end. Teachers who insist on "conclusions" are really asking students to go beyond the end. Nowhere in life is it pleasant to see people going on after they have finished; people who explain their jokes, people who linger forever at the door at the end of a visit and refuse to go home; people who have said or done all they need to do or say, and still go on puttering. In endings it may be the theatre has the edge on all other mediums of writing; if the author does not know when to end his play, the producer will find out very soon, and ring down the curtain when the audience tells him, by applause or otherwise, "That's enough."

Naturally, one would like to begin in such a way as to secure interest, attention, a receptive mood, but one must not for any cause violate the material that is to follow—and the artificial formality of introduction does just that. The first paragraph can, and in the hands of good writers generally does, set the tone of the whole piece. The first sentence can do so, as in *Pilgrim's Progress* and "The Fall of the House of Usher." The end must also leave the reader satisfied that he has not wasted his time. The beginning and end therefore are of great importance as positions of natural emphasis; but they must be, as Plato has said, integral with the whole work, and not separate pieces. The touchdown is not a separate part of the game, but the last of a series of carefully planned, successfully executed plays. The beginning of a piece of writing has similarly the importance of "first down, ten yards to go." The moment one mentions his subject he has introduced it; the moment he completes his predicate, he has concluded. The way to begin is to begin, and the way to end is to stop—and every word, sentence, and paragraph at the beginning, in the middle, and at the end should be "adapted to one another and to the whole."

This statement may seem brusque and unhelpful, but this book is not dedicated to imaginary difficulties; rather it is concerned with genuine problems which confront a writer, and there lies before us a large field to plough. If you do not know how to begin a piece, then you have not thought about it long enough, and your plan is not close to being complete. The same thing is true if you do not know when to stop.

If, after reading this section, you still have difficulty, look carefully at the beginnings and endings of essays and stories which have caught and held your attention. Here are a few examples to get you started:

On April 19, 1824, George Gordon, Lord Byron, died and went to Hell. Or did he?

It was not ugly, and in that it seemed to me to be a little less than typically Canadian.

Forty-two years ago, Lem Porteous left Winston in the middle of the night.

Dinty was a dog. Don't ask me what kind of dog; I don't know. Nobody knew.

The first two are the beginnings of essays, the third and fourth are the opening lines of short stories. Now here are a few endings:

He is, probably, wandering through space and time at this moment reciting poetry to the Wandering Jew.

Seizing a glass of beer from the nearest onlooker, she gulped it down hurriedly, lustily wiping her mouth with the back of her hand, and spoke in a loud and ringing voice. "Who's next?"
No one moved.

No, he was not carrying the chicken, but in typical, unorthodox-Dinty style, he had that hen by the neck and was making it walk!
"Yumpin' Yudas!" muttered Ole.

"That's Winston burning down," she said. "Good riddance!" Behind her, the flames rose high again, tearing noisily at the dying mill.

(7) *Punctuation*

There is no law against reading and memorizing rules of punctuation, and anyone may do so who chooses. But memory is both short-lived and fallible, and punctuation varies with every publisher and journal. The rules laid down by Harvard Press for use in their publications differ from those of Dodd, Mead & Company, and the rules of the *Atlantic Monthly* vary from those of the *Manchester*

Guardian. By accepting as final the rules of any textbook authority, the student takes his first step on the road to insanity. If he follows the rules of one press or one authority, remembering that other people do not need to conform, he may preserve his mental health.

The best thing to do is to learn what the various marks of punctuation mean, use them where and when they assist expression, and let uniformity go hang. First of all, what is punctuation? It is a collection of signals, like red and green lights and other road signs. Thus a period, which marks the end either of a sentence or of an abbreviation, says exactly what it is translated into in telegrams—"Stop!" What quotation marks, interrogation marks, exclamation marks say is obvious to anyone. We do well not to use more than one exclamation or question mark at a time. Schoolgirls who do not know how to secure emphasis otherwise are wont to put whole galaxies of marks of exclamation in their letters. Lavish use of this kind reveals both ignorance of writing skill and lack of emotional stability, expected in a schoolgirl but unforgiveable in a writer. The colon says, "Here is a list, beginning or ended. If the list has just ended, the reader knows that a summarizing statement will follow—"Cheese, apples, riding boots, and cut glass: these were his stock in trade." If no list has preceded, the colon says, "A list is coming." Thus—"His stock in trade consisted of: cheese, apples, riding boots, and cut glass." The colon also gives warning that what follows grows out of what precedes, as a consequence grows out of a general proposition, or as a conclusion grows out of a body of facts. "So it must be in writing: when the writer knows what materials to use, he will be able to draw up an intelligent plan." "It does not matter whether we are engaging in narrative, drama, poetry, or biography: the basic method is the same."

The comma says, "Don't mix." That is to say, we indicate by the comma that the words immediately separated by it are not intimately related. If we read, "A large, . . . ," the comma tells us that the word *large* does not modify the word which follows the comma, but one that will appear later. Thus in "A large, handsome dog," *large* does not modify *handsome*; it is the dog that is large and handsome. Less colloquially, the comma says, "Don't associate intimately the words separated by me; look for a larger construction." Sometimes the warning is important, as in the following: "You may take my word for it. If you don't go and see for yourself." Probably you read, "don't go" as a unit; it did not make sense; in the end you had to go back and relate "don't" properly to "take my word." Had I not intended to confuse you, I should have written, "If you don't, go and see for yourself."

The semicolon is a larger comma, dividing larger constructions. Just as commas may separate the members of a string of adjectives all modifying the same noun, so semicolons may separate co-ordinate sentences which, no longer standing alone, become clauses. When a sentence contains a great many necessary commas, it is well to see if the larger sense will not be made clearer by using semicolons in place of some of them.

If we understand the nature of the marks of punctuation, we are unlikely to get them in the wrong places, to use too few of them so our meaning becomes doubtful, or too many, freckling the face of our writing with commas. And we learn very quickly how expressive they are.

In English, punctuation is especially necessary, because we lack the multiplicity of word endings found in Latin and German, that show clearly the relationships of all parts of the sentence. We lack also the rigid systems of word order which many languages possess. With us, to neglect punctuation is to ask for trouble. The fate of many a nation has hung upon a comma. Al Capone, the Chicago ganster, spent two more years in Alcatraz because a comma appeared in the right location in his commitment papers. Dozens of examples of the value of punctuation might be produced. There is the apocryphal tale that has been told through the ages of a compliment neatly returned: Miss "A" wrote, "Miss A believes Miss B is our finest actress." The recipient put in two commas and returned the note: "Miss A, believes Miss B, is our finest actress." Then there is the old puzzle:

Every lady in the land
Has ten nails on each hand:
Five and twenty on hands and feet—
I tell you this without deceit.

Differently punctuated, the rhyme has a very different meaning. An amusing example of this device occurs in *Ralph Roister Doister*, Act III, scene iv, where Merygreke reads a love letter in such fashion he makes it seem an insult; and Shakespeare in *A Midsummer's Night's*

Dream shows Quince reciting his lines with punctuation of a kind that does similar violence to his playwright.

Punctuation really includes more than arbitrary signs. There are some words and phrases that serve the same purpose. Correlatives, as *not only*, for example, which tells us that a parallel construction is to follow, can serve the purpose just as well.

To conclude: punctuation is only a rather complicated, often personal, very necessary, Stop and Go system. Since it varies all over the English-speaking world, the best thing to do is to learn the meaning of the symbols, or at least that they have a meaning. Toward that understanding, here are a dozen examples of what punctuation can do:

1. What do you think:
I'll shave you for nothing
And give you a drink!

   What! Do you think
I'll shave you for nothing
And give you a drink?

2. The second sentence which I have omitted is too wordy.
   The second sentence, which I have omitted, is too wordy.
   [In the first, it is implied that I have omitted at least two sentences; in the second, it is implied that I have omitted only one sentence, the second one.]

3. She is a quiet, loving woman.
   She is a quiet-loving woman.

4. When we finished eating the waitress brought the bill.
   When we finished eating, the waitress brought the bill.

5. Shakespeare and other lesser poets. Shakespeare and other, lesser, poets.

6. Gossipping women are happy. Gossipping, women are happy.

7. The books which I have read I will return forthwith.
   The books, which I have read, I will return forthwith.
   [The first says I shall return only the books I have read, keeping others; the second says I shall return all the books, having read them all.]

8. We must respect our forefathers, the colonists, and pioneers.
   We must respect our forefathers, the colonists and pioneers.
   [The second says that the colonists and pioneers were our forefathers. The other lists our forefathers as a group separate from the colonists and the pioneers.]

9. Caesar entered on his head, a gleaming helmet on his feet, winged sandals at his thigh, a sword in his eye, a martial gleam.
   Caesar entered: on his head a gleaming helmet, on his feet winged sandals, on his thigh a sword, in his eye a martial gleam.
10. Woman without her man is a savage.
    Woman! Without her, man is a savage.
11. They fought for a better standard of living, more freedom, and justice.
    They fought for a better standard of living, more freedom and justice.
    [In the second, "more freedom and justice" explains the meaning of a better standard of living. In the first, they fought for three things, not one.]
12. However, attractive and artistic advertising does pay.
    However attractive and artistic, advertising does pay.

Now if you have read through these examples, and clearly understood how ingenious an instrument punctuation is, how it can in the hands of the unskilful confuse, and how, in the hands of those who understand it, it can add to and emphasize our meaning, I shall violate my own doctrine and give you a rule to memorize. And it is this: Use as little punctuation as possible, and as much as necessary. Or: Make your punctuation as meaningful as any other part of writing.

C. LANGUAGE

> "And whatsoever Adam called every living creature, that was the name thereof."
>
> *Genesis*

We have already seen something of the expressiveness of language. It will be well to pause a moment and think further of the nature of this great medium in which writers work.

Since the theory of evolution became popular there has been a tendency to ascribe actual independent bodily life to many things, as language, art, and literature, which do not grow of themselves any more than a house does, but which seem to become, as a house may, living entities. The analogy of the house is a happy one, for literature and art become our intellectual and spiritual dwelling places, and even our ivory towers, our shelters against the unknown. But the ascription of actual life to language, as it may be seen in the title of a book, "Our Living Language," is a denial of a fundamental fact of first importance, that just as men construct railways, and build houses, so men have created and are creating language.

The building of language is not something that happened only in the remote past; the instrument was not constructed and perfected by the ancients, to be passed on to us in final form. Language making is still going on, and always will go on. The human interest in it may be seen at work in every family, for all of us create our household dialects, unintelligible to outsiders. In the large, the whole human race is forever at work extending, refining, perfecting the expressiveness of speech, approximating some distant, unknown, unenvisioned ideal; and when we speak of "dead languages", we really mean, the language of dead people.

Is it really possible to progress toward an unknown ideal? Yes, of course. The rude savage, ages and ages ago, who first fastened some sort of superstructure to wheels—had he any vision of the modern automobile or railway train? So in language: down the years and the centuries it is improved by its countless users so that our own Old English seems crude and meagre compared with modern English, and the language of the Elizabethans, for all its Shakespeares or Sidneys, is creaky and awkward compared to the beauty and effectiveness to be found in English of our day.

Language is not merely the work of the whole human race, and a work in which the past and the present are contemporary and coequal; it is the greatest achievement of man. Without it, without the means of communication, no construction and no civilization is possible—not the pyramids of Egypt, neither the Suez nor the Panama canal, no medieval cathedral, no religion, no works of any art, no system of government, no steamship, railway, airplane, not even the beginnings of a modern city.

Language is the greatest achievement of man because it is the *sine qua non* of all other achievements; it is also the greatest *co-operative undertaking*. Co-operation is the most difficult of all human obligations. Otherwise, a basketball coach would not need to spend so much time trying to make a team out of five boys. Pure co-operation, co-operation that is not forced upon us by some superior authority, seems impossible on any large scale. Even an army fighting a holy war, or a war to save democracy, must hold over every individual in it the threat of a rifle shot at dawn. But in language we have on the largest scale co-operation willingly granted, and operative century after century.

Here is a word, book. What authority compels us to use that one word to denote that thing? None but common agreement. The whole process can be seen at work in any number of modern words. The inventor concocts a label from two ancient roots, and calls his invention the telephone. Other people who see and use the thing also call it a telephone, and the world calls it a telephone; there is no authority but common agreement. Another inventor calls his invention a horseless carriage; the world finds the name too cumbersome. Someone finds two other ancient roots, and by common agreement the invention is called an automobile. Even this seems too long a word now that the vehicle has become common; the tendency in England is to call it a motor, and in America a car. Who establishes these usages? All of us. The long record of our agreement is found in the dictionary, which itself has no authority, no power to lay down rules or dictate; it is permitted only to record what we in our daily walk and conversation agree upon saying. Our co-operative record is not perfect: some persons cling to old-fashioned habits, some lean toward usages which the majority of us consider vulgar, and there are some who would like to force all of us to speak as they speak, but we pay little or no attention. On the whole, we have astonishingly wide agreement concerning all matter of speech; and the record, stretching back for thousands of years, is not equalled anywhere else or in any other connection.

Many other things might be mentioned, but what can compare with the ingenious machinery of speech? It is capable of expressing the simple needs of a little child, and of elucidating the most abstruse theories of modern physics. It is equal at the same time to all the strains that may be placed upon it in the busiest streets of commerce and to those of a night of moonlight and young love. A vein of poetry runs through our most commonplace conversations; the same language when used for purposes of philosophy can be as cold and colorless as the realms of outer space. The power of words has often been sung; the subject is trite; but it is not without reason that Bulwer Lytton claimed, "The pen is mightier than the sword." The power of a slogan or catchword is well known; millions have been inflamed by a single phrase. "They shall not pass!" for example, turned an army defeated and hopeless into conquerors. "Go west, young man" inspired hundreds and thousands of the youth of two countries. No other invention of man has the universality of use and value that language has; no other invention is so powerful and so fool-proof, though many tragic misunderstandings are due to misuse of language; no other invention could be adapted to so many purposes.

I have spoken of "the ingenious machinery of speech," and must in conscience produce examples. One of the clever features we find in language is the phenomenon called ellipsis. It is *ellipsis* that clears away needless verbiage, makes speech fluent, allows us to leap trivial and unimportant gaps, and enables language to keep up to the speed of thought and the necessities of active life. Ellipsis is the trimming, the neatening, the economizing agent that makes speech so rapid that "Before you could say Jack Robinson," or "In less time than it takes to describe it," are bywords for extreme swiftness of action.

Let us look at ellipsis at work. Swift writes: "It [*The Tale of a Tub*] celebrates the Church of England as the most perfect of all others, in discipline and doctrine." Any recent writer would omit the word *others*, but the phrase as Swift has it was the regular idiom of his day and of many days before him. It is, of course, illogical; the Church of England cannot be the most perfect of all others than itself; it must be the most perfect of a group that includes itself. This illogicality was recognized, and the neatest way to avoid it was to omit *others* and leave the phrase up in the air. But when we look at what survived of the idiom, we may see that a thing cannot be the most perfect unless it is the most perfect of all, and now we find it necessary to say only, "It celebrates the Church of England as the most perfect in discipline and doctrine." Similarly, our modern word *because* derives from a phrase, *by cause that.* The Elizabethans said "because that"—as in, "Because that he ate green apples, he had a pain in his stomach." We would omit *that.*

A process similar to ellipsis, and one operative at all steps in the creation of language, is simple abbreviation or curtailment of words and phrases. Coleridge, writing of *King Lear* and referring to the attitude of Beaumont and Fletcher toward Shakespeare, says, "They miss no opportunity of sneering at the divine man, and sub-detracting from his mertis." We would say *detracting.* Thus also we have *bus* in place of *omnibus*, *phone* for *telephone*, *movies* for *moving pictures*, and a host of other curtailments. In Old English there are seven declensions of nouns, besides some sub-groups, with a multiplicity of case endings; there are also strong and weak adjectives declined in three genders with another armful of endings. Where are all the case endings now? They were a burden to the memory of speakers, and are gone. In all these curtailments, as in ellipsis, we see the paring away of excess, the neatening and trimming, of our vast and resourceful language; and with that streamlining, that shucking off of useless fat, and that insistence upon essentials, we have—as in the breeding of greyhounds, or the training of an athlete—a continually increasing beauty and grace and suppleness and verve and power.

Another clever linguistic device is the pronoun. Like all the great discoveries of man, it is so simple and obvious that we take it for granted, and never realize that there was once a time when such things did not exist. It is amazing that when the whole attention of language makers must have been fixed upon finding words to express meaning, they should have hit upon the altogether absurd device of words that express no meaning! That is what pronouns really are:—meaningless words. What does *this* mean? Or *he*, *it*, *which*? And how could anyone suppose, before they were invented, that these meaningless words would be among the most useful of all for the expression of meaning? If we could attribute their invention to any one man, he could be called, unquestionably, the greatest inventor who ever lived, but actually they are community work, and part of the blundering of mankind toward some distant linguistic perfection.

Pronouns have no meaning, in themselves, but derive their meaning from their antecedents. The word "it" can imply at one moment a tidy little Bartholomew boar pig, and the next a new hair-do, a fence post, atomic fission, or the sacrament of the Last Supper. Let us try to do without it: "We saw a tidy little Bartholomew boar pig. It was scratching its ear." Construe that second sentence without using *it*. We must not cheat by using any other pronoun. "We saw a tidy little Bartholomew boar pig. Boar pig was scratching boar pig's ear." Or we might substitute: "We saw . . . pig, scratching ear." But try this sentence: "Give me yours, and I'll give you mine." Or, "That that is, is not that that is not." Or, to be perfectly fair, take any paragraph of more than twenty-five words, and rewrite it without a single pronoun. What happens is that without pronouns our language becomes bare, elementary, and brutish, several degrees below what we condemn as pidgin English.

One of the chief glories of civilized expression is *the complex sentence*. It is made possible by the subordinating conjunction, and by the relative pronoun. Without the complex sentence, we should be unable to show the varied importance of the members of our thought; we should be reduced to the level of children.

If pronouns bring us freedom, and unimaginably extend the resources of language, they also demand responsibility in their use. The pronoun is a pro-noun, not a pro-verb, pro-adjective, or pro-incomplete-idea. Here is a sentence in which, discussing Satan of *Paradise Lost*, a student used a pronoun as a pro-adjective, or a pro-nothing: "He soon shows himself to be unrepentant, disdainful, and unconquerable in will from *which* grows a greater courage and a determination never to submit, yield, or humble himself to God." What is the antecedent of *which*? What is the noun (or noun phrase) or previous pronoun for which *which* stands in that sentence? Exactly what does the word *which* imply? Irresponsible use of pronouns is the greatest single cause of obscurity in writing.

We have illustrated the ingenuity of language by means of ellipsis and pronouns. A dozen other examples might have been used: the time mechanism of verbs, the tricks of word order, or the device of figurative expression which can take the most ordinary words of fixed and limited meaning and suddenly through them open up whole worlds of new significance. But it is not my purpose to lay bare the whole structure of language, or trace the history of English, which may be studied in many excellent books, but merely to suggest that language is a medium worthy of the love and respect of any person who works in it. We should approach it with reverence, with a determination to know it, and know it thoroughly, and with a vow that this monument to the co-operative ability, the intellectual genius of our race may not be impaired, defaced, or desecrated by our efforts; but, if possible, adorned, improved, rendered even more efficient than it now is, and passed on as the most precious heritage of those who come after. It is unlikely that any of us will ever fall upon so important a discovery as pronouns—but we do not know. Historians of the future may discern in some of our present usages the seeds of possibilities which, to us, lie far ahead, beyond our ken, and which may be one day of very great importance to mankind.

A specific word may be spoken in passing about English. It is one of the wealthiest languages, if not the wealthiest, that has ever been spoken. It lacks the universal musical quality of Italian and Spanish; it does not serve as well as French for diplomacy and abstract thought; but it is said by a distinguished expert, Otto Jesperson, a Dane, to be "a methodical, energetic, business-like and sober language, that does not care much for finery and elegance, but does care for logical consistency and is opposed to any attempt to narrowing life by police regulations and strict rules either of grammar or lexicon." Jesperson also points out that it is eminently masculine and manly.

If now this discussion of language seems labored, it is not so without reason or excuse, for it is fashionable at the moment to decry language as an indefinite or ambiguous instrument, a view which—in spite of the usual abundant list of dreadful examples—I have never been able to adopt. To me language has always seemed, in at least one sense, *an edged tool.* In the hands of an unskilled workman, it can do incalculable harm. That it can and frequently does cut and lacerate and gouge the workman himself—every teacher has his collection of "howlers"—is only proof that the man does not know how to use it.

We have already seen that part of the efficiency of language rests in words which have, quite deliberately, little or no meaning; but let us admit for the sake of argument that more exact definition of words is desirable, and that one of the purposes of men should be to achieve it. The dictionary will ultimately give us what we ask, or record what we have ourselves accomplished; and when the millenium of exact definition arrives, we shall have made a contribution to art, religion, statecraft, and science inestimably great. We shall have a perfected system of communication. All we shall then need will be scientists, statesmen, philosophers, and writers capable of using it! We have already a far more precise and exact language than Bacon had, but we have had no second Bacon. We have a far more wealthy language than Shakespeare had, but we have had no second Shakespeare.

And then, words serve various purposes. The persons who complain of the vagueness and ambiguity of language can easily find examples. If they robbed us of them, they would destroy at once many of the finest effects of literary art. When Marcellus asks in the first scene of *Hamlet*, "What, has this *thing* appear'd again tonight?" we may be sure that a more exact, specific term was at Shapespeare's command—but would such a term bring us the same sense of chill horror? Demetrius long ago remarked, "Any darkly-hinting expression is more terror-striking." It is desirable and necessary that some, indeed many, inexact words should exist. These take the edge away from sayings, as in diplomacy, which might otherwise be offensive. Sharp and cutting words can be found. Those who object to the uncertainty and indefiniteness of language are like a person who would select all the hammers and mallets from a carpenter's shop and complain that these tools won't cut.

And then, language is our own. If the mechanic can find no tool to do the precise job he requires, he will make one; and our greatest thinkers, like our feeblest, have never hesitated to coin new words. Before we enter upon the creation of new words, however—and words, moreover, which though new will be no sharper or more exact in denotation than the defining powers of their individual creators can make them—it would be only fair to readers and to those who must learn the language after us, to make sure that no effective words already exist to serve the need. Many jargon words, in education, sociology, science and, indeed, in almost all trades and professions, were made by people too ignorant of our language to know that better words to express their intended meanings were already in existence. Therefore the implied necessity is a deep and intimate knowledge of the language already in use; and it is a fair assumption that any person who gains so expert a grip upon English will have at least as much respect for it as a carver has for his chisels, or a scultpor has for his marble. He should, indeed, have that humility toward his medium of expression, and that love for it, which are essential to those who practise any art.

D. DICTION AND STYLE

> "The merit of diction is to be clear and not commonplace."
> Aristotle, *Poetics*

If language is the greatest achievement of man, the Dictionary is the most interesting book ever written. No person with any normal human curiosity can set down a dictionary at once after consulting it. It has a pull so strong that it overcomes the equally normal distaste for lists, and makes us read down pages and columns.

Why should it not be interesting? Into it is packed the entire experience of the human race. Let us take a word and make good that statement. Shakespeare shows Macbeth after the murder of Duncan crying:

> No, this my hand will rather
> The multitudinous seas incarnadine,
> making the green one red.

What a difference there is between "redden" or "make red" and "incarnadine"! Yet incarnadine means nothing more than redden.

It comes from the Latin *carnis*, and *carnis* means flesh, meat. Since raw meat and blood have a distinctive color, we use the root in the name of the flower, the carnation, bright blood red. But in modern times we also have pink carnations and white ones, and since the smell is a peculiar or individual feature of the flower, we are about to transform a color word into a word of smell. The world has forgotten the meaning of the root. Not quite forgotten, for we speak of *carnage*, which means butchery, specifically butchery of human beings who are shockingly hacked into bits of meat or flesh. Just as *carnage* means to us the last word in brutality, so *carnival* suggests the essence of merriment. Why? Because meat is not eaten in Lent, and the last meat-eating day before Lent is therefore a day on which to consume as much as possible before the fasting of the forty days. In the same way, Mardi-gras festivals and carnivals are held in many places, and mardi-gras means "fat Tuesday." After that day come six weeks of lean diet when people grow thin. But the basic meaning of Mardi-gras has been so forgotten that a group of Kansas City business men actually proposed an autumn mardi-gras. In the end they named their festival a Jubilesta. But we have not yet exhausted all the uses of the Latin *carnis*, flesh. There is a dish much favored in America today, *chile con carne*—chile, or peppers, with meat—the word coming to us this time from the Latin and Spanish. And what about *carnal* desires and appetites? Our ancestors distrusted their bodies; the flesh was vile, one of the trinity of evil set over against the Trinity of Good. They feared the World, the Flesh, and the Devil, and carnal or fleshly desires were anathema to the God-fearing. Yet our Lord, the second member of the Trinity of Good, took on the flesh, was *incarnated*; we celebrate his *Incarnation* at Christmas time. Our Lord, also, eating the Paschal Lamb at the Last Supper, was by that act a member of a *carnivorous* group. There are a number of other words sprung from this root, such as *carnify*, *carneous*, *carnose*, *carnosity*, the last a medical term to signify a malignant growth; but a more interesting one is *carnelian*, a precious stone. The term comes from an entirely separate root, and should be spelled *cornelian*, but the red color has caused confusion so that we spell it more regularly *carnelian*. Here, then, within one little group of words associated with perfume, color, butchery, fleshly appetites, and Christianity, is fixed a large part of the experience, the religious thinking, and the humor of the race.

Here is another group of some interest. *Cloth* was, at the time the King James version of the Bible was translated more than three centuries ago, the correct term for the sole garment worn by babies. It degenerated in speech to *clout*. Presently, from its somewhat disagreeable association, the word fell into disfavor. Another word had to be found for the baby's garment, and *diaper* came into general use. A wet cloth is a formidable weapon, however, so that *clout* came to mean a blow. From that usage, we have all sorts of dialectal terms, as to clout nails into the sole of a shoe, to strike, and even Lear's use of the word to mean the bull's eye, or the pin by which a target is fastened to a stake. Now the word *diaper* which replaced *clout* was the name of the finest linen used in the sixteenth century; it was an aristocratic word from the French. It very speedily lost its aristocratic air with its new associations, and gave rise to all sorts of diminutives, as *didies*, and seems now thoroughly vulgar. Its place was taken by *napkin*. Originally there was no such thing as a table napkin, nor a table cloth, but when cloths did come into use, fastidious persons wiped their hands and lips with a corner of the nap, or cloth. From that word *nap* we have *napery*, a very different word in association and meaning from the modern *sanitary napkin*, but originally, a *nap-kin* was simply a little table cloth supplied to each of the diners. Now that this word has been used in connection with the habits of babies, the tendency is to avoid it for other uses, and we speak of *serviettes* at table. Moreover, the many uses of *napkin* have dictated a change in reference to infant wear also, and some modern people speak of *cloths*, which is an interesting return to the fashion of King James's time, others of *squares*, which again returns us to *diaper* which in French meant diamond-shaped. In this group of words, we come intimately into contact with human beings and the embarrassment attendant upon their adventure into refinement.

One might go on forever, following up words to their sources, following at the same time the thinking, the psychology of the race, but this is a game which anyone can play for himself. All one needs is a dictionary and an interest in words.

That is all, and it is everything. We might speak of "wonderful windows through which we may see a dangerous coast in a dreary, most mysterious country," but Keats spoke of "Magic casements, opening on the foam of perilous seas, in faery lands forlorn." Or take a passage so perfect in itself that paraphrase of any sort would be sinful:

O, now forever
Farewell the tranquil mind! Farewell content!
Farewell the plumèd troop, and the big wars
That make ambition virtue! O, farewell!
Farewell the neighing steed and the shrill trump,
The spirit-stirring drum, th' ear-piercing fife,
The royal banner, and all quality,
Pride, pomp, and circumstance of glorious war!
And O ye mortal engines whose rude throats
Th' immortal Jove's dread clamors counterfeit,
Farewell! Othello's occupation's gone!

Sinful indeed to alter or paraphrase, to say that here a soldier says goodbye to cavalry and cannon and warfare—and suddenly a wraith of thought, of thought that is half dismay, comes flitting into the secret chambers of consciousness: the realization that once this passage did not exist, and that a very ordinary, commonplace sort of man found the perfect phrasing, the flawless rhythm, a man who had an art to learn, an "occupation" whose materials are words, and who triumphantly learned and magnificently practised it. For the man who wrote *Titus Andronicus* and the *Comedy of Errors* could not possibly have written *Hamlet* or *Othello*—but he did.

Knowledge of words, feeling for them, realization of their color and atmosphere, their nuances of meaning, make all the difference, then, between a poor writer and a good one, between competence and mastery. For the writer who knows the origin of words and their histories, who loves them, cannot but use them more carefully, more delicately, more effectively. Here are two words which mean much the same thing: *fatherly*, *paternal*. Which ought to be used when? Many similar examples might be given: *brotherly*, *fraternal; lie*, *prevaricate*, *tell an untruth; perfume*, *scent*, *reek*, *odor*, *stench; residence*, *house*, *dwelling*, *mansion*, *home;* there's no end to words that may even be almost exact synonyms, that can be defined in the same terms, but which are not the same in usage. What is the real difference between *little* and *small*? There seems to be none, yet Halsworthy has a character in *To Let*, Prosper Profond, who uses *small* in the place of *little* continually ("That's a nice small dress;" "I'm a small bit late" etc.) and the effect seems wilfully annoying.

It does not, in fact, take much ability to speak, but it takes a good deal to speak well; it takes some ability to say things, to set forth meaning, but meaning perfectly expressed requires a deft touch and superb skill. Any novice can thump the piano, even in correct time, but a musician does not merely keep time and thump. The moment he touches the keys, we are aware of overtones and undertones; sound becomes integrated, with rhythm reaching backward and forward and a unifying feeling running through the whole. In the same way, skilful writers can fire words with delightful, wicked or bitter new meaning; and they can burden them with double or triple significance all without any volation of the words themselves which mean the same afterwards as they did before.

How shocking it is to violate words which are masterpieces of the oldest art of all, the art of language-making, the one art that is universal, and to which not a few chosen persons, but all of us can contribute. How shocking, yet how common. Daily we see advertisements offering homes for sale. How can a home be bought or sold? One might as well proclaim for sale the hopes and dreams and joys, the sorrows and deeply satisfying togetherness of a family group. Homes for sale! Houses, shacks, mansions, residences, bungalows—are some things that can be sold, but surely not homes! "In Heaven," I have read in a Remembrance Day speech, "they set up their everlasting bivouac." It sounds fine, but a bivouac is a one-night stop of an army on the march; and the violation of the term transforms Heaven into less than the cheapest tourist camp—their everlasting pup-tents! *Horse*, *steed*, *charger*, *gee-gee*, *palfrey*, *mount*, *nag*, *pony*, *Percheron*, *bang-tail*, *Arab*—see how the associations, the connotations, change with the words. In matters of this sort a writer must become expert; he must not allow steeds or palfreys to haul brewery wagons.

We may mention in passing the subject of idiom, which is exceedingly interesting in English. There is no necessary logic to idiom: it is simply the habit of the language, the way we say things; and it is full of traps for the unwary. There is the old story of the chemist who put a notice in his window: "We dispense with accuracy." When a friend pointed out that the statement was equivocal, he altered it to, "We do not dispense with accuracy." Then there is the automobile sales company whose slogan warned its customers: "You'll never get a better deal," which should have induced them to look elsewhere. Some of our idioms bewilder foreigners learning our language. For example, "Good morning, Mrs. Smith. Is your husband up?" "Yes, he's up but he is not down." The adversative "but" would lead us to expect that he ought to be down when he is up. Similarly, "What does your Sandy do?" "He chops down trees." "What does he do then?" "He chops them up." Here is a perfectly correct and sensible sentence: "I could make out this tax blank if I could make it out." Think about that one. It is because idiom is tricky that dictionaries give us examples of words in use, by means of quotations; we neglect these quotations only at our peril.

How shall one learn to choose words? Any textbook of the writing art is full of helpful materials. This is one part of the art that has been well handled for hundreds of years, partly because many successful writers have left to us their suggestions concerning diction. The list is long: Chaucer, Shakespeare, Ben Jonson, Herbert Spencer, Bacon, Coleridge, Wordsworth, Samuel Johnson, and Shelley have given us helpful notes; and the great modern scholars, J. B. Greenough and G. L. Kittredge, have written one of the most fascinating books in their *Words and Their Ways in English Speech.* In addition, there are a number of students of linguistics, such as Skeat, Wyld, Sapir, and Mencken whose works are invaluable to the student of the art of writing.

The lessons of the ages may be briefly summed up. The qualities to avoid are wordiness, pomposity, inaccuracy, and triteness. It is scarcely necessary to offer examples. Students are always writing phrases such as "this modern world of today," saying that "you get as much out of education as you put in," and referring to "fields" and "phases" ad nauseam. On the other hand, the words to be chosen are the precise, the homely, the Saxon and short words, the concrete, the specific, and the imaginative. It ought to be remarked that the concrete is not one that may be picked up in the dictionary; it is any word concretely used. *Arm* is a very concrete word in itself; it is very specific in meaning; but we cannot call *the long arm of the law* a concrete or specific expression. Similarly, the imaginative word is the common word imaginatively used. A student has recently written, "From chipping out stone hatchets to harnessing of radioactive metals is a great step, but the foot is well past half way." This is what we call imaginative use of words: it revitalizes the old, worn metaphor. Another student has taken the commonplace "Let George do it" and given it new life.

Society is rapidly dividing itself into two classes: the amusers and the amused. We have an obligation to entertain ourselves, but since obligations are often distasteful, we "let George do it." Today we witness the phenomenon of women expecting George's day nurseries to shoulder the responsibility of raising their families; families paying their social obligations by asking their friends to George's night clubs; provincial governments wanting good old George, M.P., down there at Ottawa to solve the little local difficulty, and club members taking life easy while president George and his executive work their fingers to the bone.

To resume, the advice of the ages is summed up here: use words that are homely, exact, concrete, Saxon and short, and imaginative.

It is all good advice, but it cannot be taken without a caution. Homely words would be out of place in diplomatic correspondence. Nor do concrete and colorful words suit philosophical discussion. Imaginative writing does not fit in with business and workaday matters: a mortgage must not be couched in poetical terms, and the legal description of a house and lot is a very different thing from Chaucer's description of the Widow's cottage. And yet, in the experience of the ages there is still leeway enough, for Chaucer has said, "The wordes mote be cosin to the dede," and Samuel Johnson remarked, "He that thinks with more extent than another, will want words of larger meaning." The words must suit the material, and they must also suit the intended audience. A little girl once asked me, "Does a cat lay kittens?" The ensuing discussion would not have suited mature students of biology. In the same way, the language of a sermon is necessarily very different from the language of the street and market.

There is no mystery about this sort of thing. Anybody at all can learn to write. So far as diction is concerned, all that is needed is an interest in words and their values, and an ability to stand off and look at his writing coldly. This detachment will enable a writer to chop and change freely, without feeling that he is in some obscure fashion murdering himself or the offspring of his brain. Without an ability to chop and change, to revise and revise again, no one will ever learn to write, for one of the most profitable of all operations in any art is the "long labor of the file."

But let us remember, always, that it is not words that should be our primary concern, but meaning. Failure to understand this basic principle is the real reason why many persons who desire to do so, never learn to write. One young man in whom I was interested, but who never sat under me, will exemplify this point. As a beginning freshman intending to take up writing as a career, he was doing rather badly. Later in the term, I met him: "How are you doing now?" "Oh fine—all I have to do is to use a lot of little two-bit words that Mr. X can understand." It did not occur to me until afterward that Mr. X might be amused to see himself as one of his students saw him. All I could see at the moment was the blithe, insouciant face of coming failure. I tried to explain: "Mr. X doesn't want you to use two-bit words. He is not concerned about words at all. He wants you to say things, to express ideas." I was no more successful than my colleague. Is that lad a professional writer today? It is a foolish question: he tried to build his house not on the rock of unassailable principle, but upon the shifting sand of a fundamental misunderstanding.

That unassailable principle may be once more stated, this time in the words of Buffon: "To write well—it is at once to think deeply, to feel vividly, and to express clearly; it is to have at once intelligence, sensibility, and taste." The same great author says elsewhere that, "If men would only say what they have to say in plain terms, how much more eloquent they would be!" To think, to feel, and then to express. Words have no importance *in themselves*, even though we who love them come to think of them as almost living things; they are only important in that they subserve the purpose of communicating thought and feeling. They have, in a sense, no reality in themselves as they are not things, but symbols. The spoken word is a convenient substitute for the thing itself in the commerce of the world, but the written word is a symbol of a symbol, one remove further from reality.

E. EMPHASIS

> "It is of little use to have something to say, unless you know how to say it interestingly."
>
> William Archer, *Play-making*

The word *emphasis* comes to us from a Greek word which meant "significance". In modern speech the word is roughly synonymous with stress. When it is remembered that stress, though primarily vocal, is a means of indicating significance, it is justifiable to use Emphasis here to embrace methods of correctly showing the true meanings and relationships of words, sentences, paragraphs, and larger elements of writing. And it is quite likely that we have in literary criticism been somewhat confused by a multiplicity of terms used to label what is essentially the same phenomenon all through the art of writing. For the thing that is known as stress, as applied to individual words or syllables, is really the same thing that we call symmetry or proportion when speaking of larger units. A cathedral, for example, has symmetry and proportion only because the architect has known how to emphasize certain elements and how to subordinate others. An otherwise great piece of music may be ill-proportioned because the composer has not been able to subjugate one or more themes; and in sculpture, disproportion results from the same failures in stress or emphasis. One reason why photographic realism cannot be artistic is that art can never copy life exactly; there must always be heightening and shadowing, there must always be selection, there must always be varied emphasis. The first question we ask of any artist is "What do you mean?" A mere photograph has no meaning. This is not to say that there may not be art of photography, but when artistic photography occurs, there will always have been selection and arrangement of the subjects photographed; meaning will have been introduced. True realism carried to an extreme ends by becoming unrealistic, while artistic thing must always be true—and the essence of art lies in emphasis.

(1) *Emphasis by Punctuation*

Some of the means of emphasis are purely mechanical. Of these, the exclamation point heads the list, although it may frequently be merely an exterior ornament: the exclamation itself is the more genuine means of emphasis. If the phrasing is not exclamatory, the bare point serves to stereotype some of the values of the human voice and to create an exclamatory value and emphasis where another expression is possible. The following, for example, may be followed either by a period or by an exclamation mark: "She was a beautiful girl." If an exclamation mark follows, it will cause a reader to stress *girl*, or *beautiful*, or *was*. Similarly, "He hoped to control (!) his wife." The exclamation point, either within parentheses or not, fixes on the particular word a special stress, amused, satiric, or tragic. In general, exclamation marks lighten otherwise heavy or forbidding materials, and can make prosy writing seem witty, humorous, or satiric.

Since, however, the exclamation point is frequently abused, it is important to point out that any means of emphasis may be overdone. Punctuation will not save an otherwise hopeless piece of verse or prose. Nothing is so flavorless as meats too highly seasoned, and if overdoses of seasoning are necessary, readers will soon wonder about the true quality of the meat.

If the exclamation point should be sparingly used, underlining, which corresponds to italics in print, should be used hardly ever. Yet underlining can indicate the exact word to be stressed in many cases where, lacking it, there can be only ambiguity. There is a famous crux in *Hamlet:* "O cursèd spite, That ever I was born to set it right." Some actors have punched "I", others "born", and others even "set it right." What did Shakespeare mean? The discussion will no doubt go on indefinitely. Frequently the meaning of such doubtful sentences is evident in the context, but in this case the context is itself conflicting.

Whole chapters may appear in italics with special effect, and it is used in many magazines for poetry. The effect upon us may be to make the poetry seem better than it is, but we shall not be fooled in the end. Devices of this kind should be used most sparingly, for any typographical eccentricities smack of gimmickry if they do not serve directly to make meaning more clear. Another reason why these devices should be sparingly used is that they are like stimulants—they are habit-forming. The writer tends after a while to disregard better means of emphasis and to rely upon underlining and exclamation.

In so far as emphasis requires the exhibition of the proper significance and relationships of written material, all marks of punctuation also serve. For example, here are two separate sentences: "Polly put the kettle on. Sookie took it off again." If the writer wishes to imply that the sole reason Sookie took the kettle off was that Polly put it on, he may use a semicolon between the sentences, which then become co-ordinate clauses: "Polly put the kettle on; Sookie took it off again." The colon would heighten still further the suggestion of consequence, since it says, "Watch out: something coming!" If a modern system of punctuation had existed in Shakespeare's day, we would not have so many puzzling passages in his work.

Capitalizing perhaps deserves a special word. In German, nouns are still capitalized as they were for many generations in English. Gradually in English capitals were restricted to the more important nouns, and finally to proper names. However, one still finds a capital letter occasionally used for a word to which the author wishes to draw attention. One might write, "There was no question she was the Belle of the ball." The word "Belle" by this device seems to take on added significance. Thomas Carlyle greatly affected italics and capitals, and his work seems to lose some of its zest when these are stripped off. On the other hand, many readers find the device more anoying than emphatic. Compare these two versions:

So true is it, what I then said, that the Fraction of Life can be increased in value not so much by increasing your Numerator as by lessening your Denominator. Nay, unless my Algebra deceive me, Unity itself divided by Zero will give Infinity. --*Sartor Resartus*

So true is it, what I then said, that the fraction of life can be increased in value not so much by increasing your numerator as by lessening your denominator. Nay, unless my algebra deceive me, unity itself divided by zero will give infinity.

The same flattening or deflation may be seen if verse is written as prose, and many modern poets abandon capitals at the first of lines and gain thereby a visual effect in which the first word is not unduly emphasized.

(2) *Emphasis by Diction*

All the principles, virtues, and graces of writing inter-depend. If one knows how to punctuate, if one really knows, he knows how to write. If one knows how to use words, he knows how to emphasize, and if one understands either Diction or Emphasis, he has all the equipment a writer needs. Under Diction we have already discussed [I-D], at least by implication, some of the means of emphasis, since one may secure emphasis by using a stronger rather than a weaker word. It is emphatic to call a man a liar; he is less likely to reply with his fists if we say that he is a prevaricator, or hint that he has little regard for the truth. So, always. As we have seen, the strong word in English is likely to be short, specific, and concrete, rather than vague or abstract. *Luck* is a stronger word than *fortune*, *delay* than *procrastination*, *light* than *illumination*, *object* than *expostulate*.

A special form of emphasis, that might receive a chapter by itself, is emphasis by multiplication. When Samuel Johnson speaks of "troubles and commotions" he is using two words that mean, to him, the same thing. So in our common expression, "The whole kit and caboodle." We could as well say, "All of them," or "The whole kit of them." In the beginning, the phrase was "the whole kit and boodle," but the use of alliteration for emphasis is so evident in the folk mind that the word "boodle" became "caboodle."

Language provides special forms for emphatic assertion, especially —as might be expected—in verbs where the "do" forms leave no question. "I do insist" is intended to be more emphatic than simply "I insist." Since these forms violate brevity, they frequently spoil their purpose, and may die out. The point is that a wall that needs to be propped is a weak wall; by putting in a prop, we draw attention to weakness, even though the prop does make the wall stronger. It is for this reason that "very" should be sparingly used if strength of assertion is desired, for "a nice girl" is nicer than "a very nice girl." Indeed it could be said that "very" should be used with the greatest restraint, and multiples of "very" absolutely never. One's suspicions ought to increase with each "very," so that a "very, very fine day," needing so much emphasis, in fact, probably is a day fit for neither man nor beast.

We might also consider emphasis by figures of speech, but this subject will be considered in relation to imagery. It will be enough to point out here that the student who wrote that Shelley's *Adonais* "swishes with the draperies of an unreal world" had little to learn about the value of imagery. He was dressing up his thought to make it look like something—but the ideas were worthy of the costume. Similarly, Byron in *Childe Harold* wanted to say, "In spite of opposition, freedom will prevail." How could he arrest attention, make us realize the importance of this statement? Even in literature, fine feathers make fine birds, and he clothes the idea in imagery:

> Yet, Freedom! yet thy banner, torn, but flying,
> Streams like a thunder-storm, against the wind.

But literature, like life, needs fine feathers only for special occasions; we do not need evening gowns to wash dishes and sweep the floor; a too striking image may actually spoil a good piece of homespun writing.

(3) *Emphasis by Repetition*

With the assembling of words into sentences, the means of emphasis multiply. The devices already noted can still be used, but some others are usable only in sentences and larger units. If the exclamation point is emphatic, for example, so is the exclamation itself. If Hamlet had said, "I am a rogue and peasant slave," the statement well might be considered matter of fact—as matter of fact as the statement, "I live in London." We could alter the effect of it by an exclamation mark instead of a period. Shakespeare did not leave the effect of that line to punctuation; he has, "Oh, what a rogue and peasant slave am I!" The exclamation mark is hardly necessary at all and, in fact, it is modern and was not available to Shakespeare. As exclamation, the line is no longer matter of fact; it is matter of self-disgust. Carlyle, who loved acrobatics, frequently in the same way gives overwhelming emphasis to an idea: "Produce! Produce! Were it but the pitifullest infinitesimal fraction of a Product, produce it, in God's name!" People do get tired of fire-crackers all day long, and the warning should be repeated that as exclamation is the easiest form of emphasis, it becomes excessively wearisome, if not silly, when overdone.

The rhetorical question is also impossible until words grow into sentences. It is part of the stock in trade of Cicero, and of many authors, and especially of speakers. A device more acclimatized to English is the deliberate under-statement used with devastating force occasionally by Winston Churchill. Still another device capable of being used in sentences, paragraphs, or chapters, is climactic order which will be discussed presently as well as later in connection with Suspense [Part II F], for such is the intermingling of the qualities of writing that it is difficult to decide whether suspense is some element of emphasis, or emphasis an element of suspense.

Less doubt darkens our way when we discuss emphasis by repetition. It has already been seen in that exclamation of Carlyle's, and other examples might be selected from the most quoted portions of the world's literature: "O my son Absolom, my son, my son Absclom! Would God I had died for thee, O Absolom, my son, my son!" The human fact is that grief does express itself in repetition, and so do wonder, ecstasy, and other human moods. We shall now better understand that expression of Lincoln's: "Government of the people, by the people, for the people." The statement is fundamentally emotional, but held in by iron restraint. The climactic order is also effective, but it could be retained by saying simply "of, by, and for." It is essentially the repetition of "the people" that turns the trick, for as we have seen, "Government of, by, and for the people" would not set off the idea with anything like the air of significance it deserves. Take "Give me liberty, or give me death." The repetition of the words "give me" adds to the importance of the declaration and to its passion, as is readily seen by: "Give me liberty or death." The actual meaning remains the same, but the repetition adds to its significance which, we must remember, was the original meaning of the word stress or emphasis. A dash, however, which here creates a silence or pause, would serve much the same purpose: "Give me liberty—or death," but this is only to say that all the means of emphasis serve the same purpose, and prove that punctuation is as legitimate a means as any other. Again, one might say, "Time creeps on," But Shakespeare in *Macbeth* emphasizes this basic idea and adds to it a burden of unutterable weariness by seizing upon a word that can be repeated:

> Tomorrow, and tomorrow, and tomorrow
> Creeps in this petty pace from day to day
> To the last syllable of recorded time;
> And all our yesterdays have lighted fools
> The way to dusty death.

Note that emphasis is gained here by figures of speech also, and by alliteration.

The best proof of the value of repetition is that it is used in every type of literature from simple folk ballads, children's rhymes, and aphorisms, to the highest forms of literary art. Here are some examples:

> This little pig went to market,
> This little pig stayed home;
> This little pig ate roast beef,
> This little pig got none.

> Some village Hampden that with dauntless breast
> The little tyrant of his fields withstood;
> Some mute inglorious Milton here may rest,
> Some Cromwell guiltless of his country's blood.

> If a body meet a body
> Comin' thro' the rye,
> If a body kiss a body,
> Need a body cry?

> Cannon to right of them, cannon to left of them,
> Cannon in front of them, volley'd and thunder'd.

> London bridge is falling down, falling down, falling down,
> London bridge is falling down, my fair lady.

Longer examples could fill a volume. Kipling's "If" is known to everyone, as is Poe's "Raven" with its reiterated "Nevermore!" and the whole world of burden and refrain testifies to the value of repetition for emphasis and effect. One is even reminded of the famous French prescription for good teaching: La répétition; encore la répétition; toujours la répétition!—a maxim which illustrates what it teaches.

Repetition provides one notable identifying characteristic of folk ballads.

They hadna been a week from her,
A week but barely ane,
Whan word came to the carline wife
That her three sons were gane.

They hadna been a week from her,
A week but barely three,
Whan word came to the carline wife
That her sons she'd never see.

It has been used to splendid advantage by literary men of the highest excellence:

Day after day, day after day,
We stuck, nor breath nor motion;
As idle as a painted ship
Upon a painted ocean.

It has been the orator's stand-by, and it is, in special form, the structural form of Hebrew poetry.

The Lord is my shepherd: I shall not want.
[The Lord takes care of me]
He maketh me to lie down in green pastures: "
He leadeth me beside the still waters. "
He restoreth my soul: "
He leadeth me in the paths of righteousness
for his name's sake. "
Yea, though I walk through the valley of
the shadow of death, "
I will fear no evil: for thou art with me; "
Thy rod and thy staff, they comfort me. "
Thou preparest a table before me in the
presence of mine enemies "
Thou anointest my head with oil; "
My cup runneth over. "
Surely goodness and mercy shall follow
me all the days of my life: "
And I will dwell in the house of the
Lord forever. "

Here we have nothing but the repetition through various illustrations of the same simple idea, but how effectively the thing is done! No wonder it has warmed the hearts of many generations.

What is really involved here is that "amplification" which, with numberless classified methods, formed a large part of the rhetoric of the Middle Ages—and we can afford to sneer neither at the Psalms of David nor at that body of precept which nourished the genius of Geoffrey Chaucer. It is fair to say, however, that Chaucer reached full strength only when he could treat the wooden rhetoricians with some amusement, wearing his learning lightly. Nevertheless, repetition that might be called amplification is effective not merely in poetry; without it, nobody can properly develop a paragraph, especially in material at all abstruse or difficult; and repetition of important ideas may run like theme music through chapter after chapter, section after section, of a book.

A simple and obvious repetitive device is the "tagging" of some characters in a novel so that they may be easily remembered. A silly smile or a prominent nose may be mentioned every time a particular character appears. Such characters, of course, are likely to become mere types.

A special word may be said for repetition of connectives. By this means clarity may be introduced into cloudy materials. "He sent them to me and to you," is clearer than "He sent them to you and me." Connectives, however, are among the least meaningful of words. They ought not to be repeated unless a definite gain in clarity results.

(4) *Emphasis by Position*

A second great means of larger emphasis is positional. It is a daily psychological fact that the beginning and the end of any undertaking have the greatest interest for human beings, the beginning and end of a piece of writing no less than the beginning and end of the New Year's holiday or the concoction of an Irish stew. In these positions, consequently, the writer ought to place those ideas which are most important and which he expects us to remember. Amateurs violate this principle frequently by using at the beginning and end materials foreign to the rest of the piece, with the result that such papers are always improvable by simple omission. Not long ago, one of my students found that he could greatly improve a short story that he had written, by chopping off the first thirteen pages! One special trick that appeals to many unskilful writers is that of ending with a quotation, usually poetic, which has nothing whatever to do with the subject discussed. The implication that there is virtue in poetry and strength to lean upon may be refreshing, but the first lesson a writer must learn is independence, to say his say and be done.

In sentences, the commonest violations of positional emphasis occur when mere connectives are honored with the beginning and ending positions, when sentences begin with "however" and end with prepositions. These stripling words receive when so placed far more emphasis than they can bear, an emphasis out of proportion to their value in the communication of meaning. The rule is not inviolable; it is more idiomatic, sometimes, to end a sentence with a preposition. "He knew what I was thinking of" is easy and natural; "He knew of what I was thinking" is stilted and stiff.

One may also deliberately place an unimportant word in the most emphatic position, as in the following sentence: "Naturally, the real meaning of a sentence may be entirely changed by altering the order of words in it." "Naturally", in that position, apologizes—as if the author said, "I hesitate to mention such an obvious and well-known thing."

In English we have great freedom in the ordering of materials in the sentence, a freedom not available to users of other languages; but with it there goes a corresponding responsibility, since in language as elsewhere freedom and duty are complementary. Here is a joke that could be duplicated in no other language; it highlights the absence from English of limiting inflections:

Joe Kelly keeps this place.
This place keeps Joe Kelly.

Word order, it would seem, cannot be neglected in English.

Ripley found a hundred ways of saying Dante's line: "All hope abandon ye who enter here." Some of them are as follows:

All ye who enter here, abandon hope.
Abandon ye all hope, who enter here.
Abandon here all hope, ye who enter.

As Joe Kelly knew, the sense does vary with the varying emphasis. Almost the same number of variants could be derived from any simple English sentence containing the same number of words;

our freedom is amazing. Gray's line, "The plowman homeward plods his weary way," in its present form emphasizes the human element and the weariness. If it were arranged differently, it would have slightly varying meaning.

> Homeward the plowman plods his weary way.
> His weary way homeward the plowman plods.
> The plowman plods homeward his weary way.

A hundred variants could no doubt be worked out, but with slight variations in meaning as well as in word order.

From the principle of positional emphasis we may derive that the order of climax, of increasing interest, is more effective than the reverse order or any higgledy-piggledy disorder. Yet we often see an article built in this fashion: "The most important . . . . Next . . . . Next . . . ." To write in this way is to request readers to stop reading. It is especially bad when the whole structure of an essay is given away at the beginning, as in the following example: "A good teacher must be a model to his students, familiar with his subject, and devoted to his work." Every reader knows at once that there will be a paragraph or section expanding each of these items; and even if the style and diction are unusually brilliant, the writer has still thrown away his best opportunity. In difficult expository matter, or in research articles, it may be wise for the sake of clearness and intelligibility to give readers this crutch to hobble with, but certainly not in writing intended for enjoyment.

Emphasis by position will include inversions of the normal word order. "He laughed a loud laugh" has some emphasis by reason of the alliteration and repetition, but the actual line reads, "A loud laugh laughed he." The inversion underlines the effect. The natural, normal order of English speech starts with the subject, preceded by its modifiers. The verb follows, preceded by its modifiers. We say, "A trim, breath-taking girl rapidly approached me." If the positions were altered, the qualities of the girl may be stressed: "A girl, trim, breath-taking" or "Trim, breath-taking, a girl," or "There approached me a girl, trim, breath-taking." We can easily find any number of examples of inversion, or ring the changes in our own sentences. As inversion creates artificiality when over-used, there are limits to its effective use in prose, and even in poetry, where a little more licence, but very little, is permitted by reason of the exigencies of rhyme and metre.

These very exigencies mean that verse is an excellent training ground for prose writers. The limits set by a form like the sonnet, the strict requirements, compel a writer to examine every word and idea in detail, sharpen his appreciation of his own meaning, and show him the potentialities of language.

Positional emphasis may be gained by the co-ordination and subordination of materials, and by use of balance and parallelism, as well as antithesis and contrast. There is little strength in the use of the multiple "and" of childhood. "My father bought a horse and he paid sixty dollars for it and it was strong and it kicked the stable man in the leg and broke it." When some of the parts are subordinate, others receive greater emphasis, and the true meaning of the writer becomes clearer: "My father bought a horse for which he paid sixty dollars. As the horse was not only strong, but vicious, it kicked the stable man and broke his leg." Or, "My father bought a vicious horse for sixty dollars; but it was false economy, seeing that part of the price was a broken leg for the stable man." Again, the exact sense of a statement may be altered, much in the fashion of Joe Kelly and his restaurant, by shifting the subordination: "As he was given to drink, his marriage was unsuccessful," and "As his marriage was unsuccessful, he was given to drink." In either case, a point is made; but to say that "He was a drinking man and his marriage was unsuccessful" may be to fog the issue.

A last type of emphasis by position is emphasis by isolation. A single word isolated from the sentence or paragraph, from the flow of writing, will take upon itself as much emphasis as a rock standing in mid-stream. For example: "Of all his sons and daughters, grandsons and grand-daughters, the one he loved most was Cora. Cora. Cora with her bright tresses, Cora with her impudence, her vivacity." Or, "He preached and James listened. He preached the brotherhood of man, charity and forgiveness, the necessity for peace. James listened, and in his mind one word grew, at first as small as a man's hand, finally covering his whole mental horizon: Rubbish." In the last example is the effect of climax, of surprise, but it is, essentially, isolation of the word "rubbish" that turns the trick. A sentence may be isolated from a paragraph to create similar interesting effects. A student has written: "It was autumn, and during the long days Miss Winter . . ." and so on through the length of a paragraph. I do not like that use of personification, really an example of amateurish refusal to say plain things plainly; nevertheless, if that first statement were isolated, set off as a separate sentence, the whole would gain in power: "It was autumn. Miss Winter . . ." If the first sentence were set off further as a separate paragraph, it would carry little shock effect, making the background for the coming description of winter stand out.

There is also involved here an omission or silence value. Another example will show a similar effect when the expected *and* is omitted. "They were being surrounded slowly, methodically." Silence, as I have pointed out elsewhere ["Shakespeare's Use of Silence," *Transactions of the Royal Society of Canada*, Third Series, Volume XLV, 1951, pp. 59 to 81.], has powerful values for the dramatist, simply because it is the last thing expected in a play. A good example is the end of Barrie's "The Old Lady Shows Her Medals," when the Old Lady is alone and silent on the stage for a prolonged period before the curtain is lowered. The effect is very moving. Elsewhere the same effects can be gained as when one leads up to an expected climax—and then lets the reader supply his own conclusion.

While we deal here necessarily with briefer units of writing, to permit illustration, let us not forget that position, climactic order, reversed order, and isolation are of still greater importance in more lengthy works. We should not forget when dealing with sentences that paragraphs, stories, chapters, plays, and books are, like sentences, Declarative, Imperative, Interrogative, and Exclamatory in character. The true qualities of writing are the same all through, whatever the size of the unit considered; and, as we have seen, Frank Stockton's "The Lady or the Tiger," like many medieval debates, is just as interrogative as the question, "Who stole my hat?" In the same way, all the means of emphasis give strength and comeliness to the large as well as to the small.

(5) *Emphasis by Parallelism*

The use of balance and parallelism was probably best exploited in English literature by Sir Francis Bacon:

Studies serve for delight, for ornament, and for ability. Their chief use for delight, is in privateness and retiring; for ornament is in the discourse; and for ability, is in the judgment and disposition of business. . . . Crafty men contemn studies; simple men admire them; and wise men use them: for they teach not their own use;

but that is a wisdom without them, and above them, won by observation. Read not to contradict and confute; nor to believe and take for granted; nor to find talk and discourse; but to weigh and consider.

Part of the value of emphasis by parallelism is due to rhythm—part to recurrent expectation in long passages, as with the expected rhyme in poetry. A similar emphasis may be gained by a run of strong accents in the line or sentence—that is, an emphasis dependent on rhythm, or upon an expectation established, and perhaps cheated. In this respect the work of A. E. Housman is notable; and W. B. Yeats's "Lake Isle of Innisfree," with its almost complete monotony, accents the homesickness of the description. By a similar succession of the strong beats, as well as by onomatopoeia, Masefield in "Cargoes" can emphasize the lack of romance in the modern vessel: "Dirty British coaster with a salt-caked smoke-stack."

Emphasis by contrast is really an inverted emphasis by parallelism. From this method also "Cargoes" derives strength. To it may be ascribed the value of the short, sudden, sharp, unexpected sentence in the midst of longer rhythms. It jerks. Another essential contrast is the startling statement, loved by Victor Hugo. We are to have, for example, a chapter detailing Jean Valjean's escape from his pursuers, in the midst of an exciting adventure story. Hugo begins: "Paris casts twenty-five millions of francs annually into the sea." Nothing could be less expected, but this shock to a thrifty people may make them read further, and it emphasizes the manner of Valjean's escape—through the sewers. If the startling statement fails to startle, the writer deserves our pity. He will have lost his grip on his readers. Moreover, after a very few shocks we become immune and bored.

Emphasis by antithesis is wrapped up with emphasis by balance and parallelism, and may be clearly seen at work in Bacon. In longer works when it becomes large or structural, especially in drama, it has multiple effects—as also in music. The work of Haydn, for example, is full of antithetical and unexpected meanings.

(6) *Emphasis by Added Comment*

Emphasis may also be secured by added or inserted comment. The elder preachers were full of this device: "Mark my words," "Make no mistake about it," "Beyond the peradventure of a doubt." These partake of extraneous ornament, and should therefore be sparingly used: the best emphasis lies in the proper ordering of the material itself. A certain amount of trim, or outer ornament, as in architecture, may be permissible so long as the ornament does not exist for its own sake—and then, we demand a great deal of readers if every word of our writing must be carefully weighed and considered. I may write:

Since writing represents the flow of thought through concept after concept, we must be firm and sure of the concepts themselves.

This may not seem to a teacher—that is, to one who knows by experience that attention is never steady, but a matter of fits and starts—striking or emphatic enough; it does not allow the receiver a rest before being required to grapple with the gist of the matter. Therefore, I put in another phrase which is simply a sign post, a pointing finger, supplying at the same time emphasis and relaxation:

Since writing represents the flow of thought through concept after concept, we must, *as a fundamental necessity*, be firm and sure of the concepts themselves, *of the precise meaning of words, their possible meanings and associations.*

This clarification by added comment is certainly an excellent means of emphasis. The danger involved is that of becoming unbearably dry and schoolmarmish, and writing as if readers had no brains. And then, if I felt comment is necessary for clarity, I ought to go back, and find the right, the unmistakeable alternative.

Emphasis by added comment may include emphasis by illustration. The danger, as every teacher knows, is that readers may remember the illustration or be distracted by it, and forget the thing illustrated. C. E. Montague, a writer very skilful indeed, is in the following example unfortunate: "... each word is like some small parcel of earth that once was Caesar's brain and may yet make the brain of the next Christ that comes." In reading this sentence, we must first be distracted by the echo of Hamlet in the graveyard, tracing "the noble dust of Alexander till he finds it stopping a bung-hole," and then, "the next Christ that comes" stirs a question about Montague's own religion. By this time, we have forgotten that he is talking about words! The illustration overwhelms the subject, blots it from sight. Yet it is intended to emphasize and enhance.

Similarly, in *The Mad Woman of Chaillot* by Giraudoux, some financiers in the first scene brag about their gains in manipulating the markets, while, at the side of the stage, a clown juggles colored balls. The clown is an excellent comment and illustration, but the theatre effect is to concentrate audience attention upon him, and take it away from the financiers. No audience can be expected to take in that the juggler is only an illustration, for they do not even hear the financiers.

Now, we are always enjoined to write vividly, and so we should, but it must be apparent that vividness can defeat itself and the main purpose of writing. Illustrations should illustrate; they do not exist for themselves, but for a purpose beyond and greater than themselves; they must not steal the show. They should grow out of the material, should not be distracting or far-fetched; they should be servants bringing needed help, not imperious mistresses taking everything into their own hands and out of the grip of the writer. This lesson every poet, especially, should learn; for it is possible to be led by meretricious illustration further and further from sense.

It will be evident, to repeat once more, that emphasis consists in the correct ordering of materials and ideas to bring out the exact meaning of the author. In planning the whole work from the beginning correct ordering and logical distribution of material, comely proportions, ought to be a large part of the writer's preoccupation; and it ought to be still more his care when it comes to polishing the completed work. In the end, he ought to be sure that every sentence can be read in one way and one way only, and that no two people will understand the same passage differently. Someone said that the easy writing makes for damned hard reading; the converse is also true, and easy reading is likely to be due to the zeal with which the writer has checked and rechecked every chapter, paragraph, sentence, word, and comma. Easy reading is not necessarily the reading of childish materials. The thorniest, most complicated matters can be made easy by writers who are willing to take the pains; correct emphasis, due ordering and arranging of materials, no matter how difficult the idea may be, renders it lucid.

It is even possible to maintain, as Quiller-Couch does, at least by implication, that correct emphasis is the same thing as good manners. It arises out of a desire to be clearly, precisely, easily, and unmistakeably understood by those who are kind enough to read or to listen. And if we exert ourselves to make the time pass pleasantly for those who are guests in our houses, we should do at least as much for readers or hearers.

It should be added, perhaps, that emphasis can be distorted a hundred ways to create humor—and that distorted emphasis can create unconscious humor. Or, to say it in a word, the job of the writer is to direct and control the thinking of his readers—and he should not ever lose control.

A final caution may be added, if indeed it has not been stressed already: Don't over-emphasize. Don't strain for effect, for reserve begets genuine and permanent virtues. The news reporter who wrote: "A soldier of France spoke to the soldiers of Canada here Friday and with the gleaming bayonets of a famous regiment as a sounding board, sent a salute to his country's allies across the seas," had attempted emphasis by repetition in the first phrases, emphasis by showy words such as *gleaming* and *famous*, and emphasis by figures of speech. "Famous" seems an exaggeration—the actual regiment was named later; the figure of speech is absurd. The bayonets probably gleamed only inside their scabbards, on the soldiers' hips, but even if they were fixed on rifles, how could they form up into a sounding board over the speaker's head? Even "salute" is not beyond cavil, for the main sense is that of a physical gesture which cannot be sent overseas; it is not equivalent to "salutation." The passage is characteristic of that insistence upon spicing up the news, which is especially to be observed during the last war. Here, again, is a student who is to be commended except that he is slightly over-doing things: "His nose protruded from a battle-ground of rugged lines of sorrow, laughter, and meditation as a knoll would project itself from a sunburned plain." We must always remember Hamlet's advice to the players: "Anything so overdone is from the purpose." It is the purpose we must appeal to as the proper criterion and dictator of all emphasis.

This point I would like to hammer home, repeat, and re-emphasize over and over again; but I shall content myself with expressing it once more only, this time by means of an illustration: "Well, I've often seen a cat without a grin," thought Alice; "but a grin without a cat! It's the most curious thing I ever saw in all my life." Now Alice was not a literary critic. If she had been, she would not have been so astonished: she would have seen emphasis emphasizing nothing, bombast, exaggeration, "fine writing," illustrations for their own sake, grins without cats, whole zoos of them, every day trying to hide the vacuity of presumptuous speakers and writers. Let us write otherwise—with cats behind the grins.

CONCLUSION

> "If the prophet had bid thee do some great thing, wouldest thou not have done it?"
>
> *2 Kings, v:13.*

After playing with woodworking for some years and making tables, chairs, and other pieces, I found myself anxious to create a very complicated round occasional table, a maze of angles, and felt that I needed instruction. Providence sent me to a wise instructor who agreed to help. The first thing he did was to toss me a block of pine, about ten inches by four by two, and ask me to square it. So elementary and childish a task seemed absurd, but I found it exasperatingly difficult. Before I had planed that block down to the size of a lump of sugar, I had learned enough about woodworking to gaze upon all my previous efforts with shame.

Is the moral far to seek? We must always start at the beginning and it is just as important to get rid of bad methods as it is to get hold of good ones. The beginning, as far as writing is concerned, is a true conception of what is involved. How can we know the true from the false? It is a hard question, yet there are criteria: for one thing, truth is generally simple, obvious once it has been pointed out, and unglamorous.

Next, the writer must know what he is trying to do. All writing is an outward manifestation of a mental or spiritual idea, shape, or design; it is a spatial representation of a mental operation, flow or sequence. The printed page is a mirror which, miraculously, holds an image which the mind has created, and does not let it escape when the mind has gone on to other things. If there is no mental image, it cannot be mirrored; if there is no movement of thought, it cannot be represented. In a very real sense, writing is thinking.

Finally, the world has never known an expert craftsman who did not respect his tools and love the materials he wrought. The lesson, to those who wish to learn to write, must be clear and inescapable—and even more advanced writers may well question whether such simple and elementary lessons as have been provided in this, Part I, would not serve their needs also.

Part II The Virtues of Writing

"The valued file distinguishes."
Macbeth

At the beginning of Part I, Significance was set down as the fundamental law of writing, and the chapters following took the truth of that law for granted. If significance is not a prime requisite of writing, it is pointless to be concerned about diction or the ordering of materials. But when we ask, assuming that writing must be meaningful, what is necessary to a clear recognition by the reader of the meaning intended, we are obliged to demand expert use of words, careful sentence and paragraph structure, and precise emphasis. In a sense, there is nothing more to learn, and to go further is only to draw out the implications of what has already been said. If, then, we do go on to examine the qualities of good writing, we shall have an immediate test of the value or authenticity of any qualities proposed: they should be deducible from the Law of Significance.

There is a further test in the Law of the Indivisibility of Art. When we say that writing must be significant, we are saying no more than must be said also for painting, music, sculpture, and every one of the other arts. The truth is that "All art is one, whether you are carving the wood for the pulpit or preaching from it." The arts must speak to the world single and united in purpose and function, and in methods parallel. It follows that any virtue, any grace or principle should be evident in more than one of the fine arts; and if we wish to claim any quality as workmanlike and effective in the practice of writing, we must realize that we are making at the same time a larger claim.

Finally, there is the test of universality or pervasiveness. The quality proposed must be important all through the art, no matter how little or how large a specimen be considered. The quality of water is evident in the drop or in the barrel; and in writing, a quality that has virtue in it should have similar virtue whether the specimen considered be a book or a sentence, and whether the writing be philosophic, poetic, dramatic, or what not.

Confining ourselves, then, to qualities that may be called workmanlike in writing, and omitting those that belong to a higher skill, those that I believe will successfully meet these tests are: Brevity and Simplicity or Chastity, Comparison and Contrast, Variety, Activity, Significant Detail, and Suspense.

A caution may be added: there is no *desideratum* of writing, not even Significance itself, that may not be effective when deliberately disregarded or used in reverse. Humor, indeed, depends largely upon such violation, for the world of the humorist is a topsy-turvydom of things upside down and wrong end to. Even elsewhere, by deliberate exploitation of qualities reversed, writers may achieve effect otherwise impossible. So true is this statement that it almost affords a fourth test of the authenticity of the principles and qualities of writing.

A. BREVITY AND SIMPLICITY

> "Simplicity has always been held to be a mark of truth; it is also a mark of genius."
> *Schopenhauer*

"Brevity," says Polonius who does not exemplify it, "is the soul of wit." The soul! The world has accepted the statement as proverbial. That it is true becomes evident when one remembers how large a part of the effect of humor depends upon suddenness and surprise. But the word *wit* is by no means restricted to humor; its synonyms include mind, intellect, understanding, and cleverness. If the proverb is true, it must be true concerning all the products of the human intellect. And it is precisely and universally true. Stated in the form of a theorem, the virtue of Brevity, or Economy, or Simplicity, or Chastity is this: the effect of art increases in strength in direct ratio to the brevity or economy of the means by which it is created.

It is for this reason that a Gettysburg Address is capable of appealing to whole generations, while a two-hour speech may be very quickly forgotten. It is for this reason that the poems of A. E. Housman have such poignant value. It is for this reason that Greek architecture, with its chaste simplicity, outlasts the ages. It is for this reason that the American skyscraper, with its clean lines and lack of scrolls and flub-dubbery, never wearies the beholder. Caesar's *Commentaries*, wherein whole campaigns are concentrated in a few pages, are still studied in the schools, after twenty centuries, and everybody can quote some passages--if nothing else, "All Gaul is divided into three parts." And it is for this reason that those passages in prose and verse which are most strongly moving, which remain longest in the memory, are likely to be those which are briefest and simplest.

Further confirmation of the value of this element in writing may be seen in the fact that a very large part of the experience of the folk is to be found in proverbs which are short, pithy, direct, and simple. In some cases we know the history of individual proverbs and can see how they have been successively abbreviated by succeeding ages. They may have other virtues, it is true, besides Brevity: a whole course in the art of writing could be built up out of a study of proverbs alone, for all the graces of writing, and all the virtues and principles, are beautifully illustrated by them. How great and varied in their applicability; how much they say, in how little a space!

> Barking dogs never bite.
> An ounce of prevention is worth a pound of cure.
> Make haste slowly.
> Look before you leap.
> Haste makes waste.
> The nearer the bone the sweeter the meat.
> Never run after a street car or a woman—
>   there'll be another along in a minute.
> Empty barrels make the most noise.
> A ring around the finger is worth two around the tub.

If, as has often been pointed out, individual proverbs contradict others, their value as material for the study of writing is not less for that. Are not books, poems, plays contradictory of each other? Is not life itself, upon which proverbs and literature alike are based, self-contradictory?

These proverbs, then, contain the practical lore of human beings; they are derived from life. In former ages they were important in that they enabled the folk to learn wisdom by means other than direct experience. There had to be nurture whereby old heads could grow on young shoulders. It was therefore necessary that the pithy sayings be memorable; that once heard, a particular one would stick. To their purpose they are supremely adapted, being altogether lacking in extraneous ornament, but not in ornament, and in being swift and sure, pointed. This is not to say, of course, that a string of such aphorisms, or that writing that is purely sententious in character, will conform to the requirements of the highest art; but it is to say that the fundamental virtue of proverbs is equally important in any type of writing. That fundamental virtue is pith, economy, brevity.

I am not saying that, since a long work can be summarized in a few sentences, the book which can be so summarized is too long. One could never become a first class mariner by memorizing the sailor's rhyme, but that rhyme was, perhaps, a convenient, aphoristic summary of seamanship:

Red sky at night:
Sailor's delight;
Red sky at morning:
Sailor take warning.

There had to be more than this before a man could trust his weather-knowledge; he had also to know when the generalization was valueless.

Red to red and green to green,
Always let your light be seen.
When in danger or in doubt,
Always keep a sharp look-out.

Fine! But the landlubber could not steer a ship into port without a great deal more knowledge than this. He could, however, avoid making a fool of himself in an emergency.

Similarly, we may sum up in a single sentence the whole meaning of Darwin's *Origin of Species*. The title itself is half the summary.

But the full proof of his contention not only justified the expenditure of several hundred pages; it demanded them. If Darwin had put into his book, however, discursive materials not germane to the full proof, we could well accuse him of being not sufficiently brief or direct, and his book have suffered by the fault. Good writing, then, is writing whose paths are straight, whose lines converge on the meaning of the whole. There is no continual flying off at tangents, however ornamental these may be, no excursions and no bypaths, but the whole message is told directly, simply, with economy of means.

Every virtue of writing is capable of deliberate violation and will be effective in reverse. This is precisely the technique of Laurence Sterne—brevity violated. Both *A Sentimental Journey* and *Tristram Shandy* are discursive, tangential, sheer avalanches of wild words; their virtue is that Sterne never sticks to the subject, any subject. Indeed, he once remarked that, if he himself knew what he was going to write, he couldn't write it. Perhaps the character of these delightful books may best be indicated by saying that in the *Life and Opinions of Tristram Shandy, Gentleman*, the hero is not even born until well on in the third volume, and when Sterne gives over his project, after half a dozen volumes, Tristram is hardly out of his swaddling clothes. The student of writing is warned, however, that it takes an experienced hand to violate any of the principles of writing and thereby achieve mastery. The clown has to know how to do the acrobatics right before he can do them wrong.

The virtue of brevity lends strength, as it should, if it is a genuine virtue, to every individual element of writing. Parasitic adjectives, adverbs, and modifying phrases clutter up the meaning of a writer, and destroy his strength; indeed, wherever five words do the work of three, four of two, three of one, the writing is the weaker for that reason. A short sentence has natural strength, just as a short piece of timber has. A two-by-four timber four feet long will support itself and the weight of a man, while a sixteen-footpiece, of the same dimension, will not. If we must write long sentences, we must make sure that their structure lends increased strength, but it is obvious that parastic words, unnecessary to the meaning, do not add strength, but undermine such strength as might have been present without them. There is no reason why a writer could not say, "This modern world of today," if he chooses, except that unconscious repetition of the same idea in different words is uneconomic, and that the more words there are, standing between the reader and a meaning, the more difficult it is for him to burrow through the rubbish and get at the sense. If however, it were important for the reader to retain the idea of modernity, the writer could well emphasize by *deliberate* repetition: "This modern world, the world of today." Deliberate and emphatic repetition is one thing; mere words quite another.

One of the best ways to abbreviate and simplify is to cut out jargon, to write in homely, brief terms, rather than in sesquipedalian pomposity. For an excellent discussion of the topic, students should read Quiller-Couch's essay, "On Jargon," and take it to heart. Even minor abbreviations will help. Here is a sentence which is awkward because of the vague reference to "this":

> Hamlet returned home to find that his father had been murdered, that his mother had married his uncle, and his own life was in danger, and the result of all this was that Hamlet lost his interest in life.

Merely to omit "of all this" would improve the statement; further abbreviation would improve it even more. Here is a sentence from a research project on spelling:

> Statistical comparisons of the audio-vocal-visual development of comparable groups according to age and socio-economic status criteria tended to show only peripheral imbalance of perceptual skills.

Would anyone suspect that what the author means is that poor children read, and presumably spell, as well as rich ones? Or try to get the meaning out of this:

> It is fitting at this time, when we are gathered together in a group here and now, that we should not leave to the future considerations of earlier action which might have a bearing not only today but in the coming months ahead, but rather that we should bend every immediate attention to bear its light on such aspects of the problems as tend to bear heavily on the shoulders of those who may not realize which horn of the dilemma is likely to bear fruit.

It is hardly likely that the agricultural expert who was speaking really expected to harvest fruit from the horns of a dilemma, but he must have intended to say something in this sentence!

Here is the first version of an essay written by one of my students, followed by a revised version of the same passage:

Through the course of a story one usually develops an opinion of the characters therein. We find that the barber in Ring Lardner's "Haircut" ridicules or judges other people. An example is in the part where he makes fun of Milt Sheppard's Adam's apple. Having a rude sense of humor and gossipping, the barber impresses us, very vividly, with his degraded personality. We notice that his barber shop seems to harbor the idlers of the town. He has a rude sense of humor and possesses no sympathy for persons less fortunate than himself; this leads us to classify him as a coarse emotional person. An example, taken from the story, shows that he could have helped Mrs. Kendall when she took her children to go to the circus, but he preferred to stand and laugh. The language he uses doesn't exactly seem to attract us to him. These facts, however important they may appear, should not lead us to form an exacting opinion, because every individual must have some virtues to offset his defects.

* * * * * *

Like other characters in fiction, the barber in Ring Lardner's "Haircut" reveals himself. His language does not make him attractive to us, but his barber shop does attract the idlers of the town. He judges and ridicules other people, as when he makes fun of Milt Sheppard's Adam's apple. But when he stands on the side and laughs at Mrs. Kendall and her children instead of helping them to go to the circus, we feel that he is worse than a mere gossip with a crude and stupid sense of humor; he has no sympathy with the unfortunate. Perhaps we should not condemn him offhand, for every individual must have some virtues to offset his defects.

One would not claim that the second version is a deathless piece of English prose, but it will be significant that errors in English and awkard expressions tend to disappear with abbreviation.

Here is a passage from a student essay, which may be used as an exercise:

In the case of doctors, lawyers, and commercial graduates, if they are given the necessary business or professional training while at the University, they will know how to treat various cases that come before them for the first time and hence be successful during their first few years of business while their untrained fellows are experimenting often without success and are therefore losing a practice or business that might have been theirs if they had only known before they went into business, although of course experience is also a great teacher.

And here is a passage expressing an idea not more complicated. It was written by a poor fellow who never had the advantage of a freshman course in Composition, not even so much as a glimpse at the riches of this book, yet he somehow manages to make himself understood. He is Sir Philip Sydney, and he writes to a servant suspected of prying:

Few words are best: if ever I know you do as much as read any letter I write to my father, without his commandment or my consent, I will thrust my dagger into you. And trust to it, for I speak it in earnest. In the meantime, farewell.

We may detect here one of the psychological reasons for the vigor that comes with brevity: when a man speaks tersely, we know that he means what he says. But he cannot mean what he says until he knows what he means; and since it is the duty of all of us to know what we mean and where we stand, brevity affords a discipline not to be neglected.

Brevity compliments the reader—and the reader should be a full partner in the game of writing. Is not the following an insult to anyone who can read?

In this passage Richard III compares himself to Pontius Pilate, the official who is Biblically connected with the death and crucifixion of Jesus.

Misguided persons in all ages have been anxious to gild refined gold, failing to realize that true grace and power spring from simplicity. Here is a passage from the King James Bible, and the same passage rewritten, and supposedly improved, some two hundred years ago:

> Charity suffereth long, and is kind; charity envieth not; charity vaunteth not itself, is not puffed up,
>
> Doth not behave itself unseemly, seeketh not her own, is not easily provoked, thinketh no evil;
>
> Rejoiceth not in iniquity, but rejoiceth in the truth;
>
> Beareth all things, believeth all things, hopeth all things, endureth all things.
>
> And now abideth faith, hope, charity, these three; but the greatest of these is charity.
>
> *1 Corinthians, xiii*

> Benevolence possesses endurance to suffering, and yet Benevolence is not unduly ambitious: Benevolence is not inclined to ostentation, and is never insolent.
>
> It practices decorum; it is not privately selfish; is not hasty to seek a quarrel, is not malevolent.
>
> It is not pleased with wickedness, but is delighted by manifestations of truth.
>
> It has great patience, candor, cheerful expectation, and great strength.
>
> The exceptional virtues are in fact these: earnest belief, the expectation of good, and benevolence; but of these, benevolence is most to be desired.

Then there was the man who painted a solid mahogany cabinet with blue enamel.

One tends to think of Brevity in terms of phrase, sentence, and paragraph, but it is equally important in longer pieces. Many a book could be improved by chopping out whole chapters, and many a sermon that puts the congregation to sleep could grip attention if it were pithily expressed. Even structural elements can be so overdone that a book or an essay or a chapter shows itself big-boned and lacking in meat. The structure should be adequate to the job; we do not need a re-enforced concrete framework for a shack; but if we are building a cathedral, we shall need something better than two-by-fours.

It has been taken for granted that any serious student will have acquired the habit of re-writing. He will be in good company, in the company of Kipling, Conrad, Shakespeare, and, in general, of great writers of all ages. He will find that all the faults of style and thought —awkwardness, inexactness, as well as redundancy and tautology— will yield to abbreviation; simple boiling down will get rid of them. The resulting simplicity, providing he has anything to say at all, will bring strength and comeliness. If his subject is but to fill so many pages, he would be well advised never to re-write; and there are many books and printed articles which, if boiled down to their simplest terms, say nothing at all. These are not books we cherish. Final beauty and final truth seem indeed necessarily plain and simple in essence, for the profoundest truths can be felt by a little child, and the great discoveries of the world have been those which, once pointed out, became obvious. Or, as Schopenhauer says,

"Truth is most beautiful undraped; and the impression it makes is deep in proportion as its expression has been simple." Extraneous ornament, language flowery or bombastic, is evanescent in appeal, ephemeral; it dies and is forgotten "before one can say 'Jack Robinson.' "

Now in saying that writing should be simple as well as brief, I do not mean that it should be childish, but as simple as possible. As simple as possible, that is, consistent with a complete and true expression of the writer's meaning. A difficult philosophical or scientific explanation may be by no means simple, but it may be as simple as possible within the limits of the material and its due expression. This is a very different thing from the practice of some college students of trying to relieve dreary writing by means of a few "two-dollar" words shoe-horned in at all costs. The same students would laugh at the old-time Negro preacher who manufactured curious or outlandish terms to suit his needs as he went along—but they would laugh at their betters, for the preacher at least had something to say. The serious student will heed the advice of Friar Laurence to Romeo: "Be plain, good son, and homely in thy drift." His writing will become simple, brief, chaste; he will achieve all effects with the utmost economy of all means consistent with their achievement.

He will find further reward. In particular, the habit of brief and simple expression is a standing defence against that besetting sin of all artists, sentimentality. A writer who has cultivated a pithy style is less likely than another to slop over. On the positive side, suggestion and delicacy of appeal, such as we find in the work of Katherine Mansfield, grow naturally out of Brevity, out of that fastidious rejection of all that is not essential. The best writers make us equal partners with them in the game of writing, and their silences are eloquent.

B. COMPARISON AND CONTRAST

"Shall I compare thee to a summer's day?"
Shakespeare, *Sonnet XVIII*

One of the elementary methods or modes or habits of the human mind is that of comparing and contrasting, of seeking likenesses and differences. Almost at birth we begin to distinguish between things pleasant and unpleasant, between safety and danger, between good and evil; and up to the opening grave we are forever discussing similarities and differences between people and things. Much of our pleasure in life derives from our perception of varied qualities. Rhyme in poetry needs no other defence than this, that it pleases us to recognize both the likeness and the difference. Alliteration has a similar appeal in the chime, not of like endings, but of like beginnings. In music the repeated theme or motif, coming to us with a difference of background, delights us as much as our recognition of the refrain has always delighted us in song. The most constantly used figures of speech are simile and metaphor which grow out of the perception of similarities. When we commend parallelism, balance, or antithesis in writing, we are speaking of qualities in style that grow out of our constant search for likes and unlikes.

We should expect to find comparison and contrast in all arts, and we do. In painting, after all, black is only intelligible when opposed to white, and highlights are impossible without some duller background. In architecture the arrangement of columns and windows and arches demands parallelism; and the massive weight of the main body of a Gothic cathedral is set off by the delicate tracery of the spires. So it goes: through all the activities and all the arts of human beings, we are forever at comparison and contrast. Without them, no such thing as pattern is anywhere possible. Rhythm itself, in poetry or music or dancing or life, depends upon repetition with variation—or parallelism and contrast.

In writing, parallelism and contrast can be used as the structural element in sentences, paragraphs, chapters, in the whole work of whatever length. They may be used in a thousand different ways. The hero is heroic by contrast with the villain; without Iago, then Othello is not Othello; and beauty is most beautiful only when it is in contrast to ugliness. The fiery Tybalt sets off the calm Romeo, while Romeo become desperate appears beside the conventional pretty-pretty Paris. It is against the background of the Moor and every kind of sordidness that Desdemona shines forth as the very symbol of purity and innocence; and Beatrix is Beatrix, a thing of life, swift, dainty, bewitching because Esmond is slow, sober, and serious. Everywhere in literature, character is set against character, and darkness gives us light. Read "Cargoes" by John Masefield; almost all there is in that poem is contrast and comparison. The whole message is but implied.

We need not seek, however, for comparison and contrast only in drama and poetry. It is a quality that ranges from the highest realm of literature to the commerce of every day. If we wish to speak of extreme activity or purposeless agility, we say, "Like a cat on a red hot griddle," or more recently "on a hot tin roof." When we think of profitless endeavor, we remark, "Like shearing a pig; all noise and no wool." A hopeless situation is often described in terms of a snowball.

Not only so, but all parallelism and antithesis are based upon an implied comparison or an implied contrast. Thus, "Early to bed and early to rise makes a man healthy, wealthy, and wise." Take the element of comparison out and we have, "Regular habits lead to a life of prosperity and vigor," a statement which lacks all the vividness and life of the proverb. To reverse the process, to seek analogies and contrasts for our basic ideas, may be to write well. Here is a line I would rather have written than take Quebec tomorrow, and it is the work of a failing freshman who found in it his real beginning as a student, as a functioning mind. He was writing about the Church of the Middle Ages, its oppressive tithes and extortions, and of the low existence of the poor. He was thinking at the same time of the music of the Mass, the impressive ritual and ceremony, the splendor of the cathedrals. He had to find a "like" to express what he meant, and he found it in one of Chaucer's pilgrims: "The Church of the Middle Ages was like the Wyf of Bath, tricked out in outrageous finery—and 'on her feet a pair of spores sharpe.' " That is excellent writing—and the entire effect depends upon a "like," upon a comparison and contrast.

Examples of the myriad uses of contrast are not difficult to find. In "The Raven," the dread and foreboding silence of the study is contrasted to the storm which rages outside, on the wings of which the Raven is carried to the student's lattice. The black bird sits upon the white bust. The jocular air of the student at the beginning gives way to his terrible, self-torturing earnestness at the end. In "The Eve of St. Agnes" there are the bloated revellers, mouths open of the sleepers who lie in disgusting attitudes under the tables, and the dreams of coffin worms and monsters—and there is the romance of Madeleine and Porphyro. Contrast finds its way into every stanza of "The Ancient Mariner"—indeed into every masterpiece of English Literature. It must, because the distinguishing of likeness and difference is fundamental to our thinking.

C. VARIETY

"Variety is the spice of life."
Common Proverb

One of the most charming compliments ever paid to a woman is that which Shakespeare's Enobarbus pays to Cleopatra: "Age cannot wither her, nor custom stale her infinite variety." Her infinite variety! And it is precisely the same compliment that all succeeding ages have paid Shakespeare himself. Infinite variety of plot, of character portrayal, of situation, infinite variety in rhythm and in use of language, so that it is impossible to discuss the art of writing without endlessly bringing in Shakespeare and his work.

A student of mine had been reading Sabatini. He wrote with all enthusiasm about the first book of Sabatini's that he had read: yes, the finest thing he had ever met. The second, also, was superb. In the student's last essay, he said:

"In every one of his books there is a hero who is tall, dark and mysterious; a beautiful lady who loves the villain first but is finally captivated by the hero; and a villain whom he makes you like nearly as well as the hero. I remember that I liked the first book of Sabatini's that I read, but my interest has gradually decreased until now I don't enjoy his books."

In other words, if the student is correct, Sabatini is really a one-book man, one of the formula writers, who writes his one book over and over with different labels. Like Dickens's Mr. Dick, these writers get King Charles's head into everything they write. Get the pattern of one work and we have the pattern of all: the same heroes, the same situations, the same denouements—and the worst of it is that the authors themselves may be unaware of this deadly limitation. Or is that the worst? It may be that some of them consciously, in contempt of themselves and artistry and the public, grind out shoddy that revolts their own souls. But there is only one Hamlet, only one Macbeth, one Lear, one Falstaff, one Desdemona. Shakespeare has, it is true, several studies of the same motives--ambition, for example, in Richard III, Edmund, Macbeth—but what difference there is in the handlings!

Such variety runs through all his work; it is a pervasive and consistent quality in him. It is not merely a matter of variety in character portrayal, or in plot, but in every element of writing. Examine the line which deals with Cleopatra:

1 2 3 4 5 5 3 6 7 1
Age cannot wither her, nor custom stale

The line is musical, of course, but there are actually seven different vowel sounds in it. The normal line of blank verse, containing ten syllables, can have as many as ten differing vowel sounds, but the vowel sounds of English are so limited--Webster recognizes but thirty-one—that repetition of the same sound is inevitable. Even a so mechanical test as this of many English poets would be instructive; the result could certainly establish Shakespeare as one of the few who tease into their lines the utmost variety possible. But such a test would reveal only half the picture, or less, for there is a consonantal variation also to be considered, and the single line is not, in our best poets, a self-contained or complete unit. The music of verse in skilful hands interlaces line after line, so that one iambic pentameter has no more value in itself than a single bar out of an opera. In such a piece as the following, the whole is greater by far than the sum of its parts:

> Be cheerful, sir:
> Our revels now are ended. These our actors,
> As I foretold you, were all spirits and
> Are melted into air, into thin air;
> And, like the baseless fabric of this vision,
> The snow-capp'd towers, the gorgeous palaces,
> The solemn temples, the great globe itself,
> Yea, all which it inherit, shall dissolve
> And, like this insubstantial pageant faded,
> Leave not a rack behind. We are such stuff
> As dreams are made on, and our little life
> Is rounded with a sleep.
>
> *The Tempest*, IV, i, 147 ff.

Equal variety of sound and rhythm is possible in prose. Indeed, a greater variety of rhythm may be found in prose than in verse,—but this is a subject that may well be postponed for the present. Already the multitudinous variety of Diction has been suggested, but now what further means are there of avoiding a dull monotony of style?

Even in phrasing, we are never bound to stereotype. There are several methods, for example, of associating adjectives and nouns. We may use adjectives attributively (as, A red rose), or predicatively, (as, The rose is red), or absolutely (as, Red, the rose . . .). We may vary the position of subject and verb, of verb and adverb, and of phrases within the sentence.

As we go on to larger elements of writing, the possibilities of variation naturally increase. Sentences are classified as simple or compound or complex—according to their structure. According to their rhetorical values, we call them declarative, imperative, interrogative, and exclamatory. As they exemplify or violate the principle of suspense, we call them loose, balanced, or periodic. We may, therefore, have a loose, simple, declarative sentence, or a compound, interrogative, periodic one. And so on. We may have sentences long or short, ranging from more than a hundred words down to a single one. Let some mathematician compute the possible permutations and combinations!

Like the sentence, the paragraph may be simple, compound, or complex, and all the other things we have mentioned. It may contain any number of words from one to a thousand. And with all this great variety possible, most of us are content with a bare, brutish monotony with no more range of values than there is in the howling of a coyote. Is it not as if, when we might play upon an organ with a range as wide as imagination, we preferred a jew's harp or a comb? Or rather, is it not as if an organist who could fetch from his instrument the harmonies of Bach or Rheinberger were content to dispense with the foot pedals, smash the stops right and left, discard the upper keyboard, and content himself with a single stop and a single octave? Here is such an organist:

Theodore Roosevelt

Colonel Theodore Roosevelt was a very unique figure in his generation, and he will be in the generation to come. Theodore Roosevelt was a kind man and always considerate of the other fellow whom he helped all he could. Theodore Roosevelt had much influence on the public, and because of this, "Teddy," as many called him, knew how to handle men and was always a leader among the people. Teddy Roosevelt's three favorite forms of exercise were taking long walks, playing tennis, and horseback riding.

Colonel Roosevelt was the statesman, the traveller, the writer, the soldier, the father, the husband, and the family man. In all, Theodore Roosevelt was a great man, a great patriot, and a great American.

It would be brutal to compare this description of Roosevelt with that of William the Conqueror to be found in Green's *Short History of the English People*, but be brutal and look it up. Then set both beside this passage from Carlyle's "Dante":

To me it is a most touching face; perhaps of all faces that I know, the most so. Lonely there, painted as on a vacancy, with the simple laurel wound round it; the deathless sorrow and pain, the known victory which is also death;—significant of the whole history of Dante! I think it is the mournfullest face that ever was painted from reality; an altogether tragic, heart-affecting face. There is in it, as foundation of it, the softness, tenderness, gentle affection as of a child; but all this is as if congealed into sharp contradiction, into abnegation, isolation, proud, hopeless pain. A soft, ethereal soul looking out so stern, implacable, grim-trenchant, as from imprisonment of thick-ribbed ice! . . . This is Dante: so he looks, the "voice of ten silent centuries," and sings us his "mystic, unfathomable song."

Look up the whole piece and read it aloud, as Carlyle should be read aloud, and then go back and read "Roosevelt" aloud. You will find that the student is, for all practical purposes, deaf—or, to say it more kindly, that he has not yet learned that variety is the spice of seasoned prose.

Here is a delightful paragraph by a student writer who kept his eyes open, and could express with variety the variety he saw:

If coffee be the Excuse, then smoking is the Spice which imparts the flavor to a recipe for a happily Wasted Hour. A man's smoking manner does much to reveal him. There are those who "roll their own" and in the process provide a comic relief to any gathering. There are others who are so fastidious and cautious in this bit of home-manufacture that onlookers must unconsciously tag these souls with a variety of adjectives. And what shall we say of that rare gentleman whose pack of tailor-mades is kept so close to his person that the appearance of a cigarette between his fingers has something definitely mysterious about its origin? Nor can anyone long remain ignorant of the presence of the inveterate smoker of OP's. Set a diversified group like this one smoking over cups of coffee and stimulating conversation is bound to result. Let someone become enthusiastic, even explosive, and the pause for a puff on a cigarette, and the subsequent mouthful of smoke, can not but mellow his tone. After a little time the immediate vicinity will be seen to relax under the spell of a thin blue haze of smoke, which must by its very nature render the discussion suitably calm and obscure. The drawing power of a Wasted Hour over coffee lies in the undisciplined ease of the conversation, a characteristic contributed to in no small way by smoking—the Spice of the recipe.

A. E. Nelson

Variety deliberately eschewed can create a special effect of monotony, as in Hemingway's "Cat in the Rain." It is worth careful study. What we have in it is variety in reverse, a deliberate use of reiteration and monotony. It is evident that the writer should always be aware of the "sound" of his writing, and should realize that different sound effects are necessary in a description of heat in the desert from those needed for the traffic of cities, or for the music of a lively, leaping mountain stream, But it will be interesting to compare Hemingway with another writer who long ago put in his writing infinite weariness, yet kept it musical and varied. Here is Ecclesiastes xii:

Remember now thy Creator in the days of thy youth, while the evil days come not, nor the years draw nigh when thou shalt say, I have no pleasure in them. While the sun, or the light, or the moon, or the stars be not darkened, nor the clouds return after the rain. In the day when the keepers of the house shall tremble, and the strong men shall bow themselves, and the grinders cease because they are few, and those that look out of the windows be darkened, and the doors shall be shut in the streets, when the sound of the grinding is low, and he shall rise up at the voice of a bird, and all the daughters of music shall be brought low; also when they shall be afraid of that which is high, and fears shall be in the way, and the almond tree shall flourish, and the grasshopper shall be a burden, and desire shall fail; because man goeth to his long home, and the mourners go about the streets.

Now it is an astonishing thing that Ecclesiastes as an artist has to tell us, simply this: that variety and monotony are not mutually inconsistent, but can travel hand in hand. We can describe a thing so as to convey an impression of insufferable emptiness and dreariness, at the same time that our actual language and style is varied and pleasing. We may turn to Edgar Allen Poe. That there is an effect of intolerable gloom about his "House of Usher" whole generations of readers testify. To what means is it due? The sentence forms and phrasing are most musically and agreeably varied; yet there is an underlying monotony of tone, a heaviness of vowel sound, and a preference for dull consonants, to say nothing of the images involved that fill the passage with gloom from beginning to end.

There is the testimony of Conrad in *Lord Jim*. In his description of the *Patna* there is a steady, resistless, onward movement—sustained, unrelenting, endless; and yet the passage is infinitely varied in sound, in length of phrase, in sentence form. It combines monotony of movement with every kind of musical variation, and with an infinite embroidery of pattern.

Now that we have learned, from Ecclesiastes, from Poe, from Conrad, as we might have learned from many others, that variety is not inconsistent even with the dreariest and most steady or monotonous of effects, turn and read again Hemingway's "Cat in the Rain." The worst is not yet. The subject happens to suit Hemingway's style, but his style everywhere is much the same. We can only conclude that, as a writer, Hemingway prefers a penny whistle when all the daughters of music are at his beck and call.

The Hemingways of this world are legion, and his imitators have succeeded in imitating his limitations, the obvious features of his style, but unlike Hemingway, they have never had anything to say.

If we have made the point that *Variety* is always possible, we must now hasten to say that unless it grows naturally out of the materials in hand, it will seem intolerably artificial, as when one can avoid using the word "sun" only by using "Old Sol," or pillages Roget for strange terms. Variety is not an extraneous ornament; it is a pervasive quality of our thinking. To cultivate variety, we must cultivate our minds.

And if we have showed that the pervasiveness of variety is a virtue of writing, can we show that it is necessary also in the highest achievements of the other arts? In dancing, is it not perpetual variation, as well as activity and loveliness, that captivates us? In music there is no life, sparkle, or brilliance in monotone. Nor do good musicians beat out rhythms tumty-tumty-tum, but they cultivate delicacy and range of touch for varied expression. As for architecture, we may rest the case with Ruskin, and his description of Saint Mark's.

We shall push fast through [the crowds] into the shadow of the pillars at the end of the "Bocca di Piazza," and then we forget them all; for between those pillars there opens a great light, and, in the midst of it, as we advance slowly, the vast tower of St. Mark seems to lift itself visibly forth from the level field of chequered stones; and, on each side, the countless arches prolong themselves into ranged symmetry, as if the rugged and irregular houses that pressed together above us in the dark alley had been struck back into sudden obedience and lovely order, and all their rude casements and broken walls had been transformed into arches charged with goodly sculpture, and fluted shafts of delicate stone.

And well may they fall back, for beyond these troops of ordered arches there rises a vision out of the earth, and all the great square seems to have opened from it in a kind of awe, that we may see it far away; a multitude of pillars and white domes, clustered into a long low pyramid of colored light; a treasure-heap it seems, partly of gold, and partly of opal and mother-of-pearl, hollowed beneath into five great vaulted porches, ceiled with fair mosaic, and beset with sculpture of alabaster, clear as amber and delicate as ivory—sculptures fantastic and involved, of palm leaves and lilies, and grapes and pomegranates, and birds clinging and fluttering among the branches, all twined together into an endless work of buds and plumes; and, in the midst of it, the solemn forms of angels, sceptred, and robed to the feet, and leaning to each other across the gates, their figures indistinct among the gleaming of the golden ground thro' the leaves beside them, interrupted and dim, like the morning light as it faded back among the branches of Eden, when first its gates were angel-guarded long ago. . . .

In this passage we can see also the mastery of control necessary to the ordering of very long sentences. In modern style, sentences tend to be much shorter, but it is a useful exercise to try longer ones to learn how the thing is done.

Let us hope the case is proved. If we can achieve infinite variety, age will not wither our writing.

Now there is, philosophically speaking, sound reason for the fascination that variety holds for us in all the arts. It is, simply, that art imitates life. Indeed, the ancients considered that literature was nothing more than Imitation, and it is the art of imitation that they invariably discuss when they speak of writing. And life is infinitely various. When it seems otherwise, "A man would die," says Bacon, and he says it with grave emphasis in his essay "Of Death,"—"A man would die, though he were neither valiant nor miserable, only upon a weariness to do the same thing so oft over and over." What keeps us all young is a sense of the genuine newness and strangeness of the world. With perennial freshness we love the "uncertain glory on an April day."

D. ACTIVITY

"Things in motion sooner catch the eye
Than what not stirs."
Troilus and Cressida

Children choose books by their broken pages. If there are many pages of conversation, and skimpy paragraphs, the book is good; if the pages are full, it is dull. Carried to its logical conclusion, this preference means that the book which never has more than one word to a line, or a book whose pages are blank, will be the world's masterpiece. As a matter of fact, books of blank pages have been published under one title or another—Advice to Back Seat Drivers; Alibis Your Wife Will Believe; and so on—although none of them has yet found a permanent place in the lists of great works.

There is, nevertheless, some reason behind the aversion which these unskilled readers show to books that are solidly printed. Conversation suggests activity, suggests that there are no dull or idle moments in the book, but that the story is lively all the way—and it is certainly one of the facts of human nature that activity does interest us. Indeed, when we wish to speak of an event as being unusually interesting, we call it dramatic—even though drama is, on the surface, nothing but conversation. A dramatic thing interests us because it is acted before our eyes. And though there is nothing so unspeakably dull and unprofitable as a bad play, or as conversation poorly handled, conversation does liven the deadliest work. For example, without the little gems of conversation, which lend it life and brilliance, such a work as Green's history, to which we have referred before, would lose a large part of its effectiveness. Turn again to the *Short History of the English People*, to Green's picture of William the Conqueror, to prove the point.

Speeches in the midst of writing have this stimulating effect upon the interest of the reader for two reasons: they suggest the presence of human beings, and they suggest activity. Now the simple fact is that to readers in general, the most interesting of all subjects are other human beings. In painting and statuary, as in daily life and gossip, human beings loom large. In any art gallery there will be hundreds on hundreds of portraits and studies of the human form, together with some landscapes and animals; but landscapes that show no sign of human life or work, and animals which are in no way related to human lives, will rarely appear. Lifeless objects, even though made by man, will nearly always be brought in from bizarre and spectacular angles of vision, as if the artist were straining to show that "These are also interesting."

Now whether human beings interest us because man is the highest artistic achievement of God, bearing the stamp of His image, and so alive with divine fire, or whether this interest in each other is a necessity for the survival of the race on earth, that it does exist cannot be gainsaid; and, foreknowing its existence, a god could have predicted the literary forms which would most attract readers: first of all, drama, in which human beings reveal themselves; next, fiction in which they are revealed; next, biography, poetry, non-fictional prose. What Green really achieves then by the conversational bits set in the solid bulk of his description of the Conqueror, is the flash of character revelation—for people do reveal themselves and their attitudes toward others when they speak.

Conversation also suggests activity in the matter, and activity is fundamentally more interesting to human beings than quiet, or rest or the static. Indeed, if all the words synonymous with "interesting" were gathered together, they would all be found to imply activity in the exciting element or in the subject matter which rouses our attention. In the same way, an animal in the woods that remains still, fades into the background and escapes the eye of the hunter; but the animal that moves, that so much as flicks an ear, draws immediate and deadly fire. So everywhere: movement catches the eye. A flowing river will hold our attention; the same river frozen over is uninteresting. An inspired teacher may hold a class against a dog, if it is not too frisky; but if a monkey enters the room, she may as well surrender. Shakespeare, who knew so well how to catch human attention, knew this principle also. Miss Carolyn F. E. Spurgeon makes it very obvious in her *Shakespeare's Imagery*, in which she demonstrates that the most notable quality of Shakespeare's imagery is movement. This entire work is worthy of the student's careful attention. The lesson we may learn, then, is that anything that gives to writing a simulated activity will confer upon it a power to grip attention.

Many a stage play will illustrate the same principle. It is, of course, possible for two men to carry on an animated conversation while both are comfortably seated and still; but the stage director would not permit such quiescence. He would have one or both of them prowling about, picking things up and setting them down, and making exaggerated gestures. Art, at a word, is not life; and even pointless movements on the stage help to keep the audience awake. Sometimes the continual hot-foot becomes ridiculous—as it does in the wooing scene of the film version of *Henry V*, with Olivier. Henry and Kate playing hide and seek among the pillars, if taken for truth, would give one a strange impression of how boy captivates girl. But that they lack feline fierceness, and speak rather than yowl, they would better represent Tom meeting Tabby.

The principles of any art are the principles of all art: outside of Literature, plenty of illustrations can be found for the principle of Activity. In sculpture, painting, architecture, the horizontal line signifies repose; the perpendicular line, aspiration; the curved line, beauty of various sorts and meaning dependent upon the position of the curve tangential to the horizontal or the perpendicular. But activity is represented by the broken or jagged line. A long, low, flat building in which the horizontal line predominates has a very different effect from the skyscraper—but the agitation of the broken line is rarely seen in architecture. It does appear in friezes—of battle scenes, for example—and in painting it is familiar, illuminating the concern and dismay expressed in the figures of Leonardo da Vinci's "Last Supper," for example, and appearing in all paintings where vigor and activity are represented. In the work of Franz Hals, who was able to "paint noise," the jagged and broken line is abundant.

In Literature also, we must look for the surest means to achieve activity in the broken line; that is to say, the short line. So short paragraphs, short phrases, short words, will be the chief means of securing an atmosphere of activity—the chief, but not the sole means. In stories of intense action, these would naturally appear and they do appear. It would be absurd to expect to find long sentences in a radio announcer's description of a prize fight or a hockey game. He uses broken sentences, phrases, short sentences, and a great predominance of short words. In all radio, for that matter, since the problem is to seize and hold the attention of a blind audience, continual activity must be the motto of the studios. Just as the silent motion pictures had to overdo gestures and facial expressions for a deaf audience, so radio must overdo vocal expression and noise. Radio drama therefore has a far greater percentage of short sentences, phrases, and broken speech than stage drama. Elsewhere than in drama, however, since people rarely converse in complete sentences, and since, in moments of excitement, they jerk out single words or phrases, vivid writing is likely to deal in clipped speech.

Similarly the present tense will create an atmosphere of excitement. The present is always the tense of drama, as it is of folk narrative. For sustained narrative, however, it breaks down.

Naturally, intense activity would be out of place in many kinds of writing. One would not care to have a beautiful pastoral scene described in prize-fight technique, or in the style of a war correspondent. This is only to say that every principle of writing must be capable of working in reverse. We have already seen that, although Variety is a quality which aids materially the value of writing, the absence of variety can achieve certain effects which every writer may at some time wish to create.

If, again, we turn to the fine arts, we shall find that repose, inactivity, is achieved, not by the jagged and interrupted rhythms, but by smooth curves. St. Gaudens' "Lincoln" and Rodin's "Thinker" have no sharp lines; they do have bulk, and a noteworthy absence of detail, a matter to be discussed later [see Part II E]. In writing, similar inactivity can be created by long words, long sentences, long paragraphs.

Music might have been used to illustrate this principle, seeing that in music we have, in this respect, technique almost an exact equivalent to that of Literature. That essence of activity, modern jazz, is nothing but broken rhythms, interrupted motifs, while that peacefulness of such a piece as St. Saens' "The Swan" is accomplished by means of long, smooth, sweeping rhythms.

To return to analysis, why is it that short sentences have so great an effect in stimulating activity? It is not only the broken line that counts, but the fact that short sentences yield a larger percentage of verbs than long ones—and verbs are the action words of speech. Similarly, there will be a greater percentage of nouns and a lower percentage of adjectives, adverbs, and conjunctions. For the greatest activity we dispense with as many of these weak words as possible, and concentrate on the strong, active, and meaningful ones.

Or, to say perhaps the same thing in another way, short sentences are active in effect because they naturally have a greater proportion of stressed syllables. The value of the stressed syllable is familiar to us in ordinary life: I remember a man terrified when he was asked, "What did you say?" Only the speaker did not ask, "What'd y' say?" in our ordinary fashion of enunciating half of our syllables or fewer; he said, "What - did - you - say?" and paralyzed the nervous system of his opponent. He did so by importing stresses. Prose passages which seem lively and exciting to us will always have more stresses than prose that puts us to sleep. A preacher I once knew *barked* at his congregation. He was very hard on the nerves, but none of his listeners slept in church.

Any other device that breaks or interrupts the normal flow of writing, or "jazzes" it up, will help to create interest. The normal rhythm of English is iambic—let us say iambic with free use of unstressed syllables. Groups of strong stressed syllables together breaking the iambs, or thrusting in trochees, because they suggest activity, because they upset the normal rhythm, will create interest. Violations of normal word order will spice the page. Short adjectives for example, tend to precede long ones; to cheat the subconscious expectancy of a reader is to keep him awake without his realizing why. Thus, we would normally say, "The bugle sent out its low wavering notes." Merely to alter the position of the adjectives is sure to jolt a little: "The bugle sent out its wavering low notes." Omit an expected "and" and create a similar effect: "She was tall, dark, willowy." But a reader might have a right to object if we plagued him with: "She was willowy, dark, tall." But matters of this sort have already been discussed [see Part I E], and may now be omitted.

An example of the value of broken rhythms, here is a bit from Dickens's *Christmas Carol:*

There never was such a goose! Bob said he didn't believe there ever was such a goose cooked. Its tenderness and flavor, size and cheapness, were the themes of universal admiration. Eked out by applesauce and mashed potatoes, it was a sufficient dinner for the whole family; indeed, as Mrs. Cratchit said with great delight (surveying one small atom of a bone upon the dish) they hadn't ate it all at last! Yet everyone had had enough, and the youngest Cratchits in particular were steeped in sage and onion to the eyebrows! But now the plates being changed by Miss Belinda, Mrs. Cratchit left the room alone—too nervous to bear witnesses—to take the pudding up, and bring it in.

Suppose it should not be done enough! Suppose it should break in turning out! Suppose somebody should have got over the wall of the backyard, and stolen it; while they were so merry with the goose—a supposition at which the two young Cratchits became livid! All sorts of horrors were supposed.

Hallo! A great deal of steam! The pudding was out of the copper. A smell like a washing day! That was the cloth. A smell like an eating house and a pastry-cook's next door to each other, with a laundress' next to that! That was the pudding! In half a minute Mrs. Cratchit entered—flushed, but smiling broadly—with the pudding, like a speckled cannon ball, so hard and firm, blazing in half of half-a-quartern of ignited brandy, and bedight with Christmas holly into the top!

The air of animation in this piece depends, essentially, upon broken rhythms, but the exclamation marks help, or the exclamations themselves—and in lively work, like that of Carlyle, it will be found that exclamations, questions, imperatives thickly stud the style.

To see the value of verbs, without broken rhythms, we can hardly do better than Kipling. In action parts of almost any of his stories, the very words seem to jump. Look up Kipling's *Toomai of the Elephants*, and then try to match Kipling's vigorous prose.

An excellent example of the deliberate manipulation of strong stresses, plus awkward sounds intended to slow up the reader, and to suggest clumsiness in the subject, may be found in "The Walrus" by C. Lloyd Morgan. In its second paragraph, in order to attain a contrasting suggestion of speed, the rhythms smooth out, strong stresses are less frequent, and the awkward sounds disappear. Again, this is a style worth careful study.

Returning now to the analogy of music, the very strong beat as in Tchaikovsky corresponds definitely to the verb in prose. It will be possible therefore to gain the effect of activity even though sentences be long, if we maintain a larger than ordinary percentage of the active verbs. Verbs in the passive voice, of course, will give just the effect the name of the voice suggests; and it is to be remembered that the verb "to be" is one of the weakest words in the language and lends its weakness to passives. The verb-studded type of activity, like the irresistible sweep of a tidal wave, is just the effect that can be found in the work of Thomas Carlyle, the Tchaikovsky of prose. There the long rhythm predominates, but with verbs of cannonading force, as in the summary of his gospel already quoted: "Produce! Produce! Were it but the pitifullest most infinitesimal fraction of a Product, produce it in Heaven's name!" The very strong vigor of his powerful mind finds outlet in writing of elemental force and resistless sweep whose energy carries the reader off his feet in its tempestuous forward movement. Even the multitudinous asides and qualifications fail to impede the headlong rush and roar of his style.

"Ach, mein Lieber!" said he once, at midnight, when we had returned from the coffee house in rather earnest talk, "it is true sublimity to dwell here. These fringes of lamplight, struggling up through smoke and thousandfold exhalation some fathoms into the ancient reign of Night, what thinks Bootes of them, as he leads his Hunting-Dogs over the Zenith in their leash of sidereal fire? That stifled hum of Midnight, when Traffic has lain down to rest; and the chariot-wheels of Vanity, still rolling here and there through distant streets, are bearing her to Halls roofed-in, and lighted to the due pitch for her; and only Vice and Misery, to prowl or to moan like nightbirds, are abroad; that hum, I say, like the stertorous, unquiet slumber of sick Life, is heard in Heaven! Oh, under what hideous coverlet of vapors, and putrefactions, and unimaginable gases, what a Fermenting-Vat lies simmering and hid! The joyful and the sorrowful are there; men are dying there, men are being born; men are praying—on the other side of a brick partition, men are cursing; and around them all is the vast, void Night. The proud Grandee still lingers in his perfumed saloons, or reposes within damask curtains; Wretchedness cowers into trucklebeds, or shivers hunger-stricken into its lair of straw: in obscure cellars, *Rouge-et-noir* languidly emits its voice-of-destiny to haggard hungry Villains; while Councilors of State sit plotting, and playing their high chess game, whereof the pawns are Men. The Lover whispers his mistress that the coach is ready; and she, full of hope and fear, glides down, to fly with him over the borders; the Thief, still more silently, sets-to his picklocks and crowbars, or lurks in wait till the watchmen first snore in their boxes. Gay mansions, with supper-rooms and dancing-rooms, are full of light and music and high-swelling hearts; but, in the Condemned Cells, the pulse of life beats tremulous and faint, and bloodshot eyes look out through the darkness, which is around and within, for the light of a stern last morning. Six men are to be hanged on the morrow: comes no hammering from the *Rabenstein*?—their gallows must even now be a-building. Upwards of five-hundred-thousand two-legged animals without feathers lie around us, in horizontal positions; their heads all in night-caps, and full of the foolishest dreams. Riot cries aloud, and staggers and swaggers in his rank dens of shame; and the Mother, with streaming hair, kneels over her pallid dying infant, whose cracked lips only her tears now moisten.—All these heaped and huddled together, with nothing but a little carpentry and masonry between them—crammed in, like salted fish in their barrel—or weltering, shall I say, like an Egyptian pitcher of tamed vipers, each struggling to get its *head above* the others: *such* work goes on under that smoke-counterpane! but I, *mein werther*, sit above it all; I am alone with the Stars."

from *Sartor Resartus*

Activity proper to the matter in hand, then, can be attained in these several ways: by short words, sentences, and paragraphs; by short and jagged rhythms; and by a preponderance of strong stresses. Heavy materials can often be unobtrusively relieved by these means. The weary river in the pulpit puts all to sleep, and the long eloquent rhythms may lull us into indifference; but one of the greatest preachers England has ever known, one who spoke his mind to Henry the Eighth and Edward the Sixth, was one who used simple, homely phrases. Can anyone sleep through this?

And now I would ask a strange question: who is the diligentest bishop and prelate in all England, that passeth all the rest in doing his office? I can tell, for I know him who he is; I know him well. But now I think I see you listening and hearkening that I should name him. There is one that passeth all the other, and is the most diligent prelate and preacher in all England. And will ye know who it is? I will tell you: it is the devil. He is the most diligent preacher of all other; he is never out of his diocese; he is never from his cure: ye shall never find him unoccupied; he is ever in his parish; he keepeth residence at all times; ye shall never find him out of the way; call for him when you will, he is ever at home; the diligentest preacher of all the realm; he is ever at his plough: no lording nor loitering can hinder him; he is ever applying his business; ye shall never find him idle, I warrant you. And his office is to hinder religion, to maintain superstition, to set up idolatry, to teach all kind of popery. Where the devil is resident and hath his plough going, there away with books, and up with candles; away with bibles, and up with beads; away with the light of the gospel, and up with the light of candles, yea, at noondays. Where the devil is resident, that he may prevail, up with all superstition and idolatry; censing, painting of images, candles, palms, ashes, holy water, and new service of man's inventing; as though man could invent a better way to honor God with than God himself hath appointed. Down with Christ's cross, up with purgatory pickpurse, up with him, the popish purgatory, I mean. Away with clothing the naked, the poor and impotent; up with decking of images, and gay garnishing of stocks and stones; up with man's traditions and his laws; down with God's tradition and His most holy word. Down with the old honor due to God, up with the new god's honor. Let all things be done in Latin,—not so much as *Memento, homo, quod cines es, et in cinerem reverteris:* "Remember, man, that thou art ashes, and into ashes shalt thou return:" which be the words that the minister speaketh unto the ignorant people, when he giveth them ashes upon

Ash-Wednesday; but it must be spoken in Latin; God's word may in no wise be translated into English.

from "*A Sermon on the Plough*," by Hugh Latimer

Here is simplicity, alliteration, repetition, and the homely word; and here is abundant activity. No man could sleep in the presence of such a preacher. The sermon may be unduly mannered, but there can be no question that the man means what he says, and knows what he means and where he stands. We do not even need to be told that he "gave his saying deed" and that when the flames surged about him tied to the stake, he cried to his companion, "Be of good comfort, Master Ridley; we shall this day light such a candle, by God's grace, in England, as I trust shall never be put out." We may discount his ancient quarrel today, but not his courage. Nor his stout individuality which demands repetition of what has been said many times in these pages: tricks of style will never make a writer. It is the man behind the words that makes them live and glow.

E. SIGNIFICANT DETAIL

"And Leah's eyes were tender, but Rachel was beautiful and well-favored." *Genesis*

In a single sentence, the Book of Genesis tells us the whole story, a story oft repeated among the children of men, and infinite in its comment on human beings. And the whole thing depends upon a single detail: "And Leah's eyes were tender." Why were they tender? But Jacob preferred the glamor of Rachel, and did not even see the treasure that was his for the asking.

Textbooks of writing sometimes make a bow in passing to what is called "concrete detail"—as if detail could possibly be abstract—or "illustrative detail"—as if detail were a trivial matter, not indispensable but in the nature of added trimming, mere illustration. But in this story of Leah and Rachel, can the details of Leah's tender eyes and Rachel's beauty be considered dispensable? Are they not, rather, the heart of the matter? I prefer to speak of Significant Detail which may, in some cases, be the whole story, and which may in other cases be less sweeping in value—but never unimportant.

Detail may be unimportant, but the term significant eliminates from discussion all gingerbread and trimming. It eliminates mere camera-eye truth to life. A police description of a man may have a value in supplying a list of features to check when we think we have the right man, but it does not help us to find the man; nothing is more commonplace than that a dozen different suspects may be picked up by the police as answering to the same description, men who vary widely in appearance and character. To an artistic description, but one man can answer. The artistic description may not say a word of the color of his eyes or hair, the exact height, or any of the plain details that appear in a passport or police description.

Here is a description of the latter sort:

Height: five feet nine inches. Eyes: brown. Forehead: medium high. Nose: medium. Mouth: small. Hair: dark brown. Face: round. Complexion: dark. Special marks: a mole under the left eye. Age: twenty-five.

Several classes of my students were unable to recognize this man who bullied them day after day, but perhaps they might be forgiven since the age had altered by several years before I first used my passport for this purpose. My wife was not so interesting to the authorities; she is described only as: "Height: five feet six inches. Eyes: grey. Hair: brown." It is of course easy to understand why she should have married me: she fell in love with that distinctive mole under the left eye; but what on earth recommended her to me? Surely nobody in his senses would marry "Height: five feet six inches. Eyes: grey, and Hair: brown." But as Mercutio tells us that even Thisbe was only a "grey eye or so," perhaps to her Pyramus my wife also may be numbered among the queens of the earth.

Here is a woman whom we might recognize at once, and anywhere:

The sharp staccato of determined heels clattered along the sidewalk outside, and Mrs. Clarendon Desmond hove into view as though on schedule—just seven minutes late. Her sails of too sheer voile, flapping uncertainly in the heavy stillness of the evening, exaggerated unnecessarily the solid hull of the school board's major frigate, while her hat, an overturned lifeboat with a blue feather stuck through its keel, dominated her greying hair and tipped over at the front, to lean precariously down the sharp angle of her nose. She entered the room with the slightly superior smile that long habit had carved into the seasoned mahogany of her face. Respectful, subservient dislike spread in ripples behind her as she made port magnificently behind the chairman's desk, and hoisted the signal that now the meeting might come to order.

What is the color of her eyes? Of her dress? What is her height? How old is she? These things do not matter. What we need in description is the distinguishing mark, the differentiating feature, the thing that makes an individual different from all others. To say a man has brown eyes is to class him with hundreds of millions of others; but if he really is an individual, he will have an individual expression or mannerism or look about him. It is the job of the artist to find this individuality and show it. If the passport authorities had so much as added, "Looks professorish" or "Has a faintly dissipated air," to my description, they would have cut down by millions the possible suspects.

Here is another description:

Whoever had coined the word "handyman," Henry thought, must have intended it as a joke to describe Willie Forman. Why right here in Peaksville there must be a hundred squeaking doors and stuck windows and crooked hinges—yes, and open gates—to prove how "handy" Willie was.

Could we mistake this man? Yet we do not have a single direct detail about his appearance.

In the art of portraiture, Chaucer is perhaps unsurpassed. Here is one of his characters:

The Miller was a stout carl, for the nones,
Ful big he was of braun, and eek of bones;
That proved wel, for over-al ther he cam,
At wrestling he wolde have alwey the ram.
He was short-sholdred, brood, a thikke knarre,
Ther nas no dore he nolde heve of harre,
Or breke it, at a renning, with his heed.
His berd as any sowe or fox was reed,
And therto brood, as though it were a spade.
Upon the cop right of his nose he hade
A werte, and thereon stood a tuft of heres
Reed as the bristles of a sowes eres;

His nose-thirls blake were and wyde.
A swerd and bokeler bar he by his syde;
His mouth as greet was as a greet forneys.
He was janglere and a goliardeys,
And that was most of sinne and harlotryes.
Wel coude he stelen corn, and tollen thryes;
And yet he had a thumbe of gold, pardee.
A whyt cote and a blew hood wered he.
A baggepype wel coude he blowe and sowne,
And therwithal he broghte us out of towne.

Prologue to *The Canterbury Tales*

One more example:

The stranger was a tall, rather heavy-set man, thirty-five perhaps, with rimless glasses beneath heavy, colorless eyebrows. His nose, thin and pointed, played centre to the faintly condescending twists at the corners of his mouth, giving him a look of insistent superiority. His unmatching jacket and trousers were razor-sharp in their creases, and just loud enough to avoid any contrast with the shiny yellow bag he took from the seat and carried into the oak-stained shadows of the hotel lobby.

It must be evident that there is a difference between detail and significant detail. For that reason, a great deal of modern literature is on the wrong track. There has been an attempt at photographic realism in many modern books. But the camera, because it can see everything, sees nothing. It sees the unimportant as well as the important, the insignificant as well as the significant, and unless there is some indication of relative significance to the reader, the result is tedious beyond words. Green, in his picture of William the Conqueror referred to before, does crowd the canvas, but since the details are important, the effect is that of a living portrait.

Vividness, in short, which is an obligation of description, is dependent almost entirely on the detail selected. In textbooks of writing it is usual to offer rules regarding description. These may or may not be of value. We are told that we should proceed from the general to the particular, sketch in the large features first, and then fill in the minor ones. We are told to begin with what is near, and go on to things that are farther off, from what one would naturally first see to what one notices later. And we must be careful to stick to a "point of view." Rules, it seems to me, are only made to be broken; and then, usually they arise out of one or two particular examples like Poe's description of Landor's cottage. Because Poe did use a certain method in selecting details and point of view in that case, must the rest of the world to the end of time follow his example? A thousand equally good methods can be found. As for beginning with what one naturally first notices, and going on to the next most noticeable feature, to do so may be to destroy all possibilities of picture-making. It may take long study to winnow out the really significant—as against "what one first notices"—from the chaff of appearance. Perhaps we ought not to lay down rules regarding the order of materials in a description, for it would be quite easy to find examples of excellent descriptions which use no order at all, but present details in a higgledy-piggledy fashion. That, indeed, is the method of the finest portrait artist in English literature, Geoffrey Chaucer. Look at the Miller: one of the last things mentioned is what we would naturally see first, his white coat and blue hood and bagpipes. Before that, we have an impression of his size, something about his habits, the color of his beard, his nose, his sword and buckler, which we would certainly have seen earlier had we been looking at him, his mouth, more about his habits. There is no order of materials here; indeed, Chaucer has gone to the extreme of separating the Miller's nose from his mouth by means of a sword and buckler. Nevertheless, it is a magnificent piece of portraiture.

As for sticking to a point of view, one may do so and freeze to death. Many motion pictures begin by showing a wide expanse of land. The camera then narrows down to a village, a house, a doorway, then a character: the point of view shifts, and it is reasonable that it should do so. It does shift gradually and rationally. Or the scene may enlarge from a character to a doorway, a village, a countryside. Or we may move the camera along road or highway. Here is one case of the moving camera technique:

The long freight clicked in slowing rhythm over the switch at the lower end of the Peaksville yard, pushed through the cobwebs of an early morning ground mist, and jerked to a stop in front of the station, its air lines leaking in weary whispers. Back at the tail end a lantern gleamed faintly, its light fading in an unequal struggle with the dawn. From a gondola twelve cars from the engine, a slim, dishevelled man slipped awkwardly to the ground, jerked a small blue dunnage bag to his shoulder, and plunged from the right of way. He hesitated momentarily as the company hedge loomed out of the mist to block his path, then swerved quickly to the left and slipped through a break in the dripping foliage. On the other side he stopped, kicked his bag under the hedge, and, almost casually, flipped tobacco and papers from the pocket of his grey flannel shirt.

From the station came the sound of a window being thrust open, and a thin, reedy voice called through the mist.

Though it was not yet half past three, the sun was already turning toward the mountains, its silver rays changing to a brilliant blending of bronze and blood red. Where the wind had carved out drifts and hummocks, the shadows had turned from grey to blue and then to a deep grey-purple that stood out in sharp contrast to the red-gold radiance on the open places. Where some other skier had passed before them, two ribbons of a brighter gold stretched far ahead to where the dark masses of evergreens marked the edge of the river valley. Above the trees the sky was pale almost to whiteness in a broad band that rested lightly on the black and silver and purple of mountains that seemed to wait a stone's throw beyond the river valley, the forty miles between river and mountain range shrunk to nothing in the clear air. Far to the left, a single plume of white smoke rose from some farmstead straight upward into the cold, motionless sky.

from *Vagrant Whistle*

There are two cautions that may be stressed regarding details. One is that the search for detail of genuine significance may lead to strain. The student who wrote, "His nose protruded from a battleground of rugged lines of sorrow, laughter, and meditation as a knoll would project itself from a sunburned plain," was perhaps less vivid than strenuous.

The second caution is this: in any work that is not of the most immediate and ephemeral value, one must be careful about contemporary references, for it is amazing how rapidly events that seem important to us become meaningless. I once wrote a lecture on the subject of college term papers, papers which report upon investigations. That was written at the time of the trial of Richard Bruno Hauptmann for the kidnapping and murder of the infant son of Charles E. Lindbergh. At that time the whole American world hung upon the day by day, even hourly, reports of the trial; school and college classes were interrupted for fresh reports; and I built up a large part of my discussion with a detailed parallelism between the trial and the necessary steps in investigation and reporting. That paper became valueless in almost no time, it seemed to me; Lindbergh himself, who had been the idol of American youth from coast to coast, was now unknown, and R. B. Hauptmann was not even a name. Through the "Now" march steadily a generation of men, and many in the swift "Tomorrow", after a dozen years, will never have heard of events which at the moment seem all-important. Now it is true that the permanent in literature must grow out of specific experience and finite detail, but contemporary events make the most ephemeral of all materials for writing.

Perhaps a further word may be added, even though it has already been said, at least by implication. General words, like beautiful—gorgeous—riot of color—handsome—have no real meaning themselves. They convey only a general impression. One specific, or significant detail has as much value as a hundred such words.

Is this principle of writing capable of working in reverse? Of course. In all art there are occasions when we may not desire to be specific—or when, if an Irish bull may say it, the details should be general. Epstein's "Day" and "Night" are simply great amorphous blobs of stone; and Michelangelo long ago showed how to paint masses of undifferentiated form. Here is Milton's description of Hell:

> At once, as far as Angels ken, he views
> The dismal situation waste and wild.
> A dungeon horrible, on all sides round,
> As one great furnace flamed; yet from those flames
> No light; but rather darkness visible
> Served only to discover sights of woe,
> Regions of sorrow, doleful shades, where peace
> And rest can never dwell, hope never comes
> That comes to all, but torture without end
> Still surges, and a fiery deluge, fed
> With ever-burning sulphur unconsumed.
>
> *Paradise Lost, Book I*

How is one to learn to manage significant detail? Obviously by study and by being interested. One must be alert to the things he writes about, familiar with them; he must know them better than anyone else does. One must build up, also, the habit of seizing impressions, cultivating them, pondering always what is really meaningful, discarding that which is not. Practice study of photographs or portraits is useful. Study a picture or a person until all the insignificant drops away and you can find one word to re-create the picture, or crystallize its meaning. Having found that word, it will be easy to pick out corroborative details. One must become Macbeth:

(Enter Servant)

MACBETH: The devil damn thee black, thou cream-fac'd loon!
Where got'st thou that goose look?
SERVANT: There is ten thousand—
MACBETH: Geese, villain?
SERVANT: Soldiers, sir.
MACBETH: Go, prick thy face, and over-red thy fear,
Thou lily-liver'd boy. What soldiers, patch?
Death of my soul! Those linen cheeks of thine
Are counsellors to fear. What soldiers, whey-face?
SERVANT: The English force, so please you.
MACBETH: Take thy face hence.

Like Macbeth, we must seize the one important detail with the swiftness of vision.

Here are some pieces of writing which will bear examination for their use of significant detail:

A. I was only a small boy, but the scene is very vivid in my memory. The cold, bitter night, with the white, even surface of the snow stretching out to a great distance; the few scattered lights on the horizon; the frosted rumps of the horses and the dull brass on the harness; the cold light of the winter stars, and the silence, and the lantern light falling on my mother's face. *Sverre Solberg*

B. She is tall, dark-haired, with a fine figure that suggests rigid foundations. Little strings of sparklers—maybe glass or maybe diamonds—dangle from her ears, making me think she's probably off to Banbury Cross. Her green cloth coat is too bright, and over her shoulders a silver-grey fox with little pointed ears and glass eyes winks at me. *J. R. Settle*

C. As the years went by, the pictures of Lem they carried in their minds faded or changed, according to their ways of thinking, and by the time I heard the story, there wasn't much anyone could be sure about, except that he was a medium little guy, with hair red enough to start a fire, and a grin so wide it seemed to hang down from his ears like a pair of spectacles. *H. V. Weekes*

D. For a moment she stood still and looked at me, her raised forearm suspended in the act of wiping her nose.

"I hear you'll be wantin' a housekeeper to neaten and do the cookin'," she said. *Anon*

E. When we happen to see an individual whose countenance is "all tranquility and smiles," who is full of good humor and pleasantry; whose manners are gentle and conciliating; who is uniformly temperate in his expressions, and punctual and just in his everyday dealings; we are apt to conclude from so fair an outside, that

"All is conscience and tender heart"

within also, and that such a one would not hurt a fly. And neither would he—without a motive.

William Hazlitt: *The Spirit of The Age*

F. SUSPENSE

"Oh, wilt thou leave me so unsatisfied!"
Romeo and Juliet

The word *suspense* comes to us from the Latin and means hanging under or over, a state of uncertainty. The essential image of the word is the sword of Damocles which hung by a hair over the unhappy victim and which might descend at any moment. Suspense consists, simply, in creating in the mind of the reader a desire for further information.

Thus, in the "Hail to the Chief" of Tannhauser the music leads us to expect the entrance of an important person. Similarly, in drama the hero of a play rarely appears at the rise of the curtain, but enters only after the curiosity of the audience has been whetted by many references to him. Naturally, if the hero is unworthy of the build-up, the device fails and causes anti-climax. The anti-climax may be intentional, as when Shakespeare, after an "alarum", a roll of drums which would lead us to expect an army, sends on the stage Falstaff solus.

All of us are familiar with the sort of suspense that we may call large, or gross, that is to be found in adventure and murder stories and in some motion pictures. But that even a sermon or a philosophical treatise may use suspense is not commonly realized. (See Latimer at the end of Part II D.) If suspense is a true quality of writing, it must be proved so in all elements of writing, and nothing is easier.

Even punctuation may aid in creating suspense, if we are correct in saying that suspense arises out of a desire for further information. Try a simple test: "She had always loved friends, fun,—". Do you not feel a little desire that this sentence be completed? Not to keep you on tenterhooks, here it is: "She had always loved friends, fun, and laughter,—". Now if the sentence had ended there with a period, you would have been satisfied, but the dash holds you up again and you want that sentence finished. Very good: "She had always loved friends, fun, and laughter—and now she lived alone." It may be pointed out in passing that "and" does not always mean "and"; it is not always merely a plus sign. In that sentence, the last "and" means that what follows is a comment on the rest.

Other marks of punctuation can help suspense, notably the colon. If I say, "The reasons why he murdered his wife were:" you will not stop reading at the colon; you will go on.

Can suspense be otherwise created in individual sentences? Of course. What do me mean by climactic order and anticlimax? We mean simply that we are playing a game with the reader; if we play it in a serious way, we create in him a desire to go on; but when we are in a humorous mood, he will not mind if we cheat his expectation. To say, "Two, four, six, —" is to create an expectancy that "eight" will follow; to say, "Two, four, six, three," is to cheat the expectancy—and, if it is done suddenly, it will make the reader smile.

Not only in climactic order, but in all manner of other ways, suspense can be created in the single sentence. It may be achieved by means as simple as the distinction between "a" and "the": "W—, a little town with the fresh air [that "the" sets up an expectancy] the quiet street, the lazily busy people, and the peculiar noises of small farm animals, was my destination." The student who wrote that sentence did not mean to speak of the fresh air of small farm animals, but he did not realize that "the" may be a promise word. It seems that students frequently neglect such words as "a" and "the" as being unimportant, but here are two sentences quite different—in meaning:

> She had always enjoyed a feeling of shelter.
> She had always enjoyed the feeling of shelter.

The first means that she had always been sheltered. The second means that she enjoyed the feeling whenever she was sheltered. Another of the promise words, frequently misused, is "so". When we see it, we expect, either an exclamation mark, or a "that" or an "as" to follow.

> She was so pretty!
> She was so pretty that she upset the boys.
> She was so pretty as to become a nuisance.

Suspense may be created, then, by promissory words.

Again, should I say, "Although he was an enormity of wickedness, Adolph Hitler —", will you not wait for me to complete the sentence? You may, but as I can't complete it, I won't! And here you smile. How do I know? How do I know, sitting at my typing table that you will infallibly smile at this point? I know because the subordinate clause sets up an expectancy of a following principal clause which will be contrary in meaning, which will adduce something to offset the wickedness attributed to Hitler. The expectation then is swiftly cheated—and surprise is a large element in the creation of humor. But the larger point is that an author can control the set of mind in his readers. It is his duty to do so; they must not be permitted to think anything but what he wants them to think.

Subordinate clauses before the principal clause contribute to suspense, as in the last example. The *correlatives* will also do so. "He was not only fierce —." Such a sentence leads us to expect the "but also"; and if a speaker stopped at this point, the audience in growing anxiety, would wait for him to drop the other boot. Many speakers take advantage of audiences in this fashion. It is said of Churchill that he would deliberately pretend to be in distress, so as to gain the full attention of his hearers, and then, follow through with one of his best periods. This is an ancient trick to which the ancients gave a name: *Hyperabaton*. Longinus says of Demosthenes: "He often begins to say something, then leaves the thought in suspense, meanwhile thrusting in between, in a position apparently foreign and unnatural, some extraneous matters, one upon another, and having, thus, made his hearers fear lest the whole discourse should break down, and *forced them into an eager sympathy with the danger of the speaker*, when he is nearly at the end of a period, he adds just at the right moment, i.e., when it is least expected, the point which they have been waiting for so long. And thus, by the very boldness and hazard of his inversions, he produces a much more astounding effect." Similarly, a drill sergeant can break the nerves of even a hardened squad by refusing to complete a command.

It will be evident that *the essence of suspense is delay.* The impeding elements, also, can be inserted in the sentence, paragraph, or longer work, at any point before the end. But, in general, the difference between a sentence which has suspense and one which has not, is simply the difference between a periodic sentence and a loose one. In the periodic sentence the meaning is not complete before the period; in the loose one, the reader can fall asleep and wake up a dozen times before the end. Or, to say it otherwise, a period could be put in at many points in a loose sentence before the end.

Loose: He lived. simply. and was happy. in a little cabin. by the river. and caught logs. which he sawed up. and sold. for firewood.

Periodic: Living simply, in a little cabin by the river, and catching logs which he sawed up and sold for firewood, he was happy.

If we give the principal clause such a build-up as this, however, it has to be a principal clause worthy of the emphasis given. "He was happy" is insufficient, a mere anticlimax.

If suspense can be created in these ways in the sentence, it is similarly created *in paragraphs*, for, as we saw in Part I B, a paragraph is simply a sentence raised to the second power. The whole texture of a piece of writing can gain in interest by the use of suspense in all its parts, for the chief difference between an interesting style and a dull one, whether the material be heavy or light, is suspense. One reason why the word "textbook" is synonymous with dullness is that textbook writers frequently write the pith of a paragraph in a single sentence, sometimes printed in italic or black face, and then proceed to explain. Topic sentence writing falls to the same curse, since the topic sentence inevitably gravitates to the beginning of the paragraph. Good writing is more expertly controlled: the writer does not permit his meaning to become complete before the last period of the last paragraph.

In elements of writing larger than paragraphs, suspense of a grosser kind is, of course, possible, but it will always be created by the same means: by stirring up a desire for information which is withheld. Some titles—"A Dream," for example—destroy suspense at once. Every reader knows that, at the end, the hero will wake up. "A Day's Outing," a favorite topic given by many teachers over the years: that is, since the time of Noah, is a crime against children. We know at once that the hero will go forth, have a good time, and come back; or he will go forth, have a bad time, and come back. "A Trip" will be read by only the most determined readers, but every year teachers everywhere add it to their sufferings.

The beginning of the story, as well as the title, is important from the point of view of suspense to be created. We may begin, as Poe does in "The Raven" and "The Fall of the House of Usher," by enlisting the aid of an atmosphere of mystery, or we may begin with a startling situation or statement that demands explanation, as Coleridge does in "The Ancient Mariner." In short stories a cryptic remark is often found at the beginning: "When Greek meets Greek, then comes the tug of war, but when a red-headed girl meets a two-fisted sergeant of the Royal North-West Mounted Police . . . ." It would be almost a relief to write "one-fisted" for a change.

Good writing always looks forward. Or, as we have said before, writing is best thought of as a stream of discourse flowing from a beginning to an end; it should not flow backward. Herein lies the unreasoned but not unreasonable prejudice of readers against references back to a title. This chapter is headed "Suspense". The first sentence reads, "The word suspense . . . ." To begin instead with, "This word . . ." would be to prejudice many readers at once. Further evidence of the forward-moving nature of writing, its cumulative principle, may be seen in anticlimax. A student has written: "He was passionately excited, frantic with fear. He was not in his normal mood." We can use exactly the same words, but alter their order, and avoid that anticlimax: "He was not in his normal mood, but passionately excited, frantic with fear."

Moreover, good writing looks forward up to the very end, and a "Thus we see" ending is an acknowledgement that the writer does not know how to complete the job. When a student writes:

> Thus we see that the wilful blindness of one man and the sentimental blindness of the other are combined by fate to bring about all these tragic deaths and complete the wheel.

he is like a horse that shies at a jump: he has failed to rise to his own climax.

There are times when the larger suspense is impossible because the audience already knows all the facts, and there are times when this larger suspense may be abandoned at once, since one may have other fish to fry. For example, Adrien Bonjour, writing about "The Use of Anticipation in *Beowulf*," [*Review of English Studies*, XVI, July 1940, pp. 290-99], shows that *Beowlf* is full of statements that indicate to the reader what the outcome of this or that incident is to be. The actors in the epic being ignorant of these outcomes, however, there is built up a sense of over-hanging fate that makes the story grisly. Like other qualities of writing, then, suspense may be effective in reverse, denied when expected.

Masefield uses these anticipations in *The Widow in the Bye Street*. Before this long poem, which ends in the execution of the Widow's son for murder, has got well started, Masefield tells us, "And all the time fate had his end prepared." Such hints come frequently through the poem. These anticipations have the effect of slowing up our reading so that we may enjoy the poem more as we go along; but being in vague terms they also stimulate us to read to the end.

In using what I have called gross suspense, the writer may come to be victim of his own tricks. It is probably impossible to get any very high literary or artistic values into a mystery story, for example, because the writer himself has created in the mind of the reader one, and only one, engrossing question: "Who did it?" and the moment the question is answered, interest is so dead that all the king's horses and all the king's men cannot bring it to life again. Nobody can remember a mystery story; and nobody would read one that is not stream-lined to the barest necessities of narrative.

But if the writer said at once: "John Henderson killed his wife at ten o'clock on the morning of August fifth," he could then go on and tell a powerfully moving story, full of artistic values, simply because he has at once surrendered all possibility of gross suspense. A most interesting example of this kind is Conrad's *Lord Jim*. After some teasing and suggestion, Conrad lets the cat out of the bag after some seventy-five pages. He is then able to go on for another hundred pages of most gripping recapitulation from several points of view, showing us the impact of the basic story on men of various character. Similarly, any reader who can get well into Browning's *The Ring and the Book* will find an amazing fascination in re-reading the same story—the same characters, the same incidents, the same situations—told many times from different points of view.

One hesitates to pick out further examples of suspense—the world is full of them—but for various reasons the following pieces will be worth analysis:

Poe: "The Pit and the Pendulum"
Coleridge: "The Ancient Mariner"
Shelley: "Ode to the West Wind"
Robert Frost: "The Death of the Hired Man"

CONCLUSION

"And Jacob served seven years for Rachel; and they seemed to him but a few days, for the love he had to her."

Genesis, 29:20

A student's first success often comes when he becomes excited about some subject. Why?

Because his lively interest will induce him to scratch beneath the surface and find better materials. It will tend to keep him to the point, brief, simple, active. It will cause him to pounce on significant elements, in his subject, even to contrast what he believes with what he denies. In animated writing there is likely to be a natural variety; and if the student is really keen, he will be building up to a climax, and not spilling all he knows in the first sentence. So long as the feeling is honest, therefore, it is good for a young writer to be angry, bored to exasperation, or excited by his subject. It is good to take materials by the neck and shake them, rip them up the middle and down the back, smash them, or fall upon them like an angry god upon a sinner.

Some students, of course, and especially girls, "emote" for too little reason. For them, restraint is necessary, the guardian of sincerity—but it is genuine feeling we are speaking of.

The reason why work full of feeling is good is that interest is infectious. Like measles or smallpox, it catches. High school youngsters can and do become interested in the most unlikely things simply because an enthusiastic teacher or classmate is interested in them. Later in this book, Enthusiasm will be discussed as one of the few indispensables of the best writing.

This enthusiasm must be real, not assumed or insincere; and it grows out of mastery of materials. Each writer must be his own real authority. "I only speak the things that I do know," says Mark Antony, whom we have already quoted. His words have corresponding effect. But no one can do well when trying to speak without knowledge, unless in the way of unconscious humor—which consists largely in effects not intended. "Under a dark, dismal, black-purple sky," a student has "blue waves tossing." On the ship she has a captain who treats the storm as no sea-captain would. Well, Melville and Conrad gained success by writing about the sea! Perfectly true, but they wrote about what they knew; both of them served long years in ocean-going sailing vessels. We shall best imitate them by writing about what WE know. It does not recommend a writer if we are obliged to say that he does not know what he is talking about.

Yet this is a criticism that can fairly be levelled at a great deal of amateur work. I have read of peonies and tulips blooming at the same time—in a story by a young writer. In a poetry contest in Missouri, two thousand miles from the nearest salt water, three-quarters of the poems dealt with the sea. The fault is not confined to young or amateur writers. "Caliban in the Coal Mines," a poem by Louis Untermeyer, is nothing but nonsense. Obviously he has never worked in coal mines; he doesn't know what he is talking about. For Untermeyer or anyone else, ignorance is a road that will not lead to excellence.

Many students, again, do their first good work when seized by ideas they cannot express. Their dispositions shake, like Hamlet's, with thoughts beyond the reaches of their souls. For that reason, I have always tried to assign difficult subjects for essays, subjects for which there are no easy, ready-made answers, to be sieved out of the common air. But man is prone to evil as the sparks fly upward: too often the result has been glib and meaningless, a straight case of refusal to meet the challenge. Even so, if no more than one of a class met the issue, found the fun there is in writing, caught a spark of the divine fire, or gained the deep satisfaction of saying well something entirely one's own, the teacher should still rejoice. His batting average would be high.

To return: Chastity, Comparison and Contrast, Variety, Activity, Significant Detail, Suspense—what do they all amount to? Simply this: no man can hope to write well so long as he is content to prattle. There must be self-discipline, and there must be knowledge of the craft. A carpenter's apprenticeship once lasted seven years. Can we expect to become writers in less time? We can be prattlers in no time at all; but for that clear and vivid expression and that burning integrity that are the glory of letters as of other arts, we must expect to labor as long as Jacob served for Rachel. Now if this seems a discouraging or a Spartan doctrine, there is yet one truth we must firmly embrace, and this is the truth that technique liberates talent; it does not kill it. The student who refuses to prattle, who refuses the easy, glib, and empty way, who believes his mind and heart were meant for more than vacuity and dust, will find himself developing in two ways. He will enrich his reading with an understanding heart and his expression with a furnished mind. And as there is no end to learning, he will remain young forever. Seven years will seem but a few days, and he may sigh with Chaucer: "The lyf so short, the craft so long to lerne."

Part III The Graces of Writing

"Grace and harmony are the sisters
and images of goodness and virtue."
Plato

Over, *above*, and *beyond* the virtues of writing which belong to the skilled craftsman, there are certain excellences, or graces, which distinguish the artist. These are the little touches which, when we notice them, bring a smile of kindling appreciation to our lips, touches like the grace notes of music or that quality in art that is known as *virtu*. In a certain sense these added graces could be called supererogatory, since they belong to that sort of technique which is more than one's money buys, extra, and indeed beyond price. It is as if one said, "For a few dollars one can buy tickets to the theatre and be permitted to watch for an evening the work of a skilled dancer; but no amount of money can possibly be said to pay for the dancing of a Pavlova."

Now, in testing the strength or virtue of craftsmanlike quality in writing, we made it a point of honor to prove their pervasive or consistent value in all the elements of composition from sentence to book. We tried also to show that the same virtues prevail in other arts. When we speak of the graces of writing, however, there is no such obligation to prove either pervasiveness or community; for we speak of minor, though important, felicities which in their nature may well be inherent in a single art, applicable within a single medium, and local in value. Every art has its graces, but single graces are not necessarily pervasive within the art or common to all arts.

For example, I can conceive of nothing in writing comparable to the advantages which a painter gains from the simple, natural fact that our eyes seek the light. One spot of light in a gloomy picture will stand out; one spot of dark in a bright picture will hardly be seen. The manipulation of light by a Rembrandt or a Rubens is not a mere matter of contrast, though the contrast is necessarily there. The fact that we see dark things with an effort of will is obvious—whereas light attracts. Before the eyes can distinguish anything else, baby will turn toward the light. Seizing upon this inherent human response to light, and appealing to it, the painter can make things inexpressibly beautiful; but to the writer, direct manipulation of light is impossible.

Similarly, the painter cannot handle time; he cannot narrate; and to him the nightingales are dumb—"There is one glory of sun, and another glory of the moon, and another glory of the stars: for one star differeth from another star in glory." Not in their fundamentals, but in their graces or virtuosities the arts are individual.

Virtuosity, however, is a subject which a teacher hesitates to discuss with young students. For if a student fails to develop some points of excellence on his own, one suspects that he never will. On the other hand, if the graces of style should become his end and aim before he has learned that the first and final, the inescapable necessity of all writing is a message to communicate, we should have the most hopeless of all evils, mere virtuosity, empty technique. Into this peril such otherwise great writers as R. L. Stevenson, Oscar Wilde, and A. C. Swinburne fell more than once, so that we have from them brilliant displays of technique in essays, poems, and dramas that say nothing. To say nothing is bad enough, but to say it with brilliant execution is to sin against one's talent. Music of this type is not fit even for finger exercises.

Two things, then, become evident: that virtuosity is easily overdone; and that it is not, in work of genuine artistic merit, a separable or unnecessary feature. Its only excuse is that it is necessary, germane to the matter, highlighting the message of the writer. The final test of the value of writing will always be its significance, and whether every word, letter, and comma contributes to that significance.

The elements of technique to be discussed in Part III are these: Alliteration, Onomatopoeia, Sense Appeal, Counterpoint, Suggestion, Irony, Imagery, and Rhythm.

A. ALLITERATION

"'rum, ram, ruf,' by lettre."
The Parson's Prologue from
The Canterbury Tales

Alliteration or initial rhyme seems to have a special appeal to Anglo-Saxons. In a standardized form, with conventions and rules, it was the structural basis of Anglo-Saxon poetry, and it endured as the basis of poetry for at least seven hundred years, more than twice the time-span from our day back to the landing of the Pilgrims. Even in Chaucer's time, poems both popular and courtly, like Gawain and the Grene Knight, Piers Plowman, to say nothing of sacred "Lives" and "Legends", were written in alliterative form, while alliterative prose was equally common, as indicated in the "Katherine Group" of Saints' Lives. The language which a man speaks from infancy till thirty may well have a charm for his ear at seventy; and alliteration still falls pleasingly on the ears of English-speaking peoples. Alliterative poems have been written in modern times, by such poets as Swinburne and Bridges, and alliteration adds a special grace to rhymed verse, blank verse, and free verse of all periods. A search for examples in poetry would bring us in a treasure trove of some of the finest poems in English. Here is one example from the rigidly proper verse of the eighteenth century:

The curfew tolls the knell of *p*arting *d*ay — p d
The *l*owing *h*erd *w*inds slowly o'er the *l*ea, — l h w l
The *p*loughman *h*omeward *p*lods his *w*eary *w*ay, — p h w p w w
And *l*eaves the *w*orld to *d*arkness and to me. — l w d

Two lines from Sandburg's "Fog"—"*O*ver *h*arbour and *c*ity/ *O*n *s*ilent *h*aunches"—(o h s ; o s h), could be taken as exactly meeting the requirements of the interlaced alliterative line of Old English poetry, while the interlacing of alliteration in Gray, though less exact in its throwback to Old English conventions, is certainly not less interesting. These, however, are isolated examples; the whole "Elegy in a Country Churchyard" will yield returns as rich as those of its first stanza, and so will the whole body of Sandburg's work. So will all modern English poetry. If any reader feels that these results arise from pure chance, let him take any paragraph of newspaper prose and hunt the letter. Or let him take any paragraph of this book. Poems that the world loves will be found full of alliteration.

The exact psychological value of alliteration is difficult to estimate. It has certainly some mnemonic value. It has emphasis. The folk have definitely sought it out in those rhymes by means of which in unlettered days the learning of the father was passed on to the son. Thus the sailor's rhyme already used:

> *R*ed to *r*ed, and *g*reen to *g*reen
> Always *l*et your *l*ight be seen.
> When in *d*anger or in *d*oubt
> Always *k*eep a sharp loo*k*-out.

Similarly, alliteration is the structural element in a great many of the popular proverbs:

> *L*ook before you *l*eap.
> A *b*ird in the hand is worth two in the *b*ush.
> *B*arking *d*ogs *d*on't *b*ite.
> *W*ilful *W*aste makes *W*oeful *W*ant.

Its mnemonic value makes it seem likely that alliteration is best in ordinary prose to point up or emphasize a crisp, definite statement, but that it has other values is evident from its use in poetry.

Like everything else, alliteration can very easily be overdone. An example of such overdoing may be seen in the work of John Lyly, and Shakespeare has satirized alliteration, along with a great deal of other nonsense, in the play of Pyramus and Thisbe in *Midsummer's Night's Dream:*

> PYRAMUS: Sweet moon, I thank thee for thy sunny beams;
> I thank thee, Moon, for shining now so bright;
> For, by thy gracious, golden, glittering gleams,
> I trust to take of truest Thisbe sight.
> But stay, O spite!
> But mark, poor knight,
> What dreadful dole is here!
> Eyes, do you see?
> How can it be?

O dainty duck, O dear!
Thy mantle good,
What, stain'd with blood!
Approach, ye Furies fell!
O Fates, Come, come,
Cut thread and thrum;
Quail, crush, conclude, and quell!

There may also be an unconscious alliteration that will spoil otherwise good work, as in an example that Stevenson spotted in Macaulay:

Meanwhile the disorders of *C*annon's *C*amp went on in*c*reasing. He *c*alled a *c*ouncil of war to *c*onsider what *c*ourse it would be advisable to ta*k*e. But as soon as the *c*ouncil had met, a preliminary *q*uestion was raised. The army was almost ex*c*lusively a Highland army. The recent vi*c*tory had been won ex*c*lusively by Highland warriors. Great chiefs who had brought si*x* or seven hundred fighting men into the field did not thin*k* it fair that they should be outvoted by gentlemen from Ireland, and from the Low *C*ountries, who bore indeed *K*ing James's *c*ommission, and were *c*alled *c*olonels and *c*aptains, but who were *c*olonels without regiments and *c*aptains without *c*ompanies.

Only the c's have been marked here, but there are subsidiary alliterations almost as bad, as "*f*ighting men in the *f*ield did not think it *f*air . . ." The moral is that we must be conscious of all the elements of writing; there are pitfalls everywhere for the unwary.

Alliteration certainly adds to the sweep and force of Ruskin in the passage we have quoted [Part II C] and generally through his work; Poe uses it freely, and Burke uses it for an occasional explosive emphasis, and it adds an unobtrusive felicity to the best pages of English prose. It will be evident that, if only for emphasis, it has genuine artistic values. Discreetly used, it pleases the ear.

It may be said, however, that in bad writers alliteration will highlight the badness already existing, while in the work of the good writers it may become another grace of style. It is definitely of importance in poetry, and in prose, it may serve as a sort of leitmotif running with inexpressible grace through a passage, and teasing the ear, and emphasizing the message. Much the same conclusions are to be made for rhyme in prose; it is useful for emphasis, and it can be unobtrusive and pleasing, but it becomes an addiction. The fact, however, that "reimproza" was one of the arts of the Middle Ages, and that rhyme appears so frequently in proverbs (rhyme and assonance) —"Haste makes waste," "A stitch in time saves nine," etc.—proves it has emphasis value.

Consciously overdone, alliteration can have a humorous effect as in O. Henry's "callosity of heart, caramels, and a congeniality for the capers of Cupid." The same value can be found in rhyme, as in the following example:

But you will be saying that Spring can't be as bad as all that. No, it isn't at all. After the initial events heralding its approach, we have more delightful weather. The grass becomes luxuriantly green. The crocusses, cactusses, and peonies all come out in bloom. God's little creatures become apparent. For instance, there are ants. And when I say ants, I mean ants, ants in the rhubarb, ants on the lawn, ants that are working, ants that yawn, ants that are happy, ants that are sad, ants that are driving me quietly mad. Of course, there is a very logical explanation.

The student who wrote that piece used his rhyme deliberately for comic effect. But here is another using rhyme seriously—and most unfortunately—in an essay about Benet's *John Brown's Body.*

Those of the South, oh why do they fight? It's because they are sure they are doing the right. They fight for the right of their state that must be free to decide its own fate. In the South they were bred, in the South they will stay, as long as the sun sheds forth a ray.

Georgia'll fight while Virginia can express the love for the state of each man. To the North, they are determined not to fawn, if their very lives they should have to pawn. They were free. They had the right of secession e'en though it caused in the land a depression.

After a few paragraphs everyone except the author has had enough of this sort of thing. He is perhaps hardly to be blamed, however, for we occasionally find bastard prose in syndicated newspaper features—and then, for perhaps the first time in his life he was captivated by a poem. If rhyme is good in such a work as *John Brown's Body*, why should it not be good in a student's essay? The answer is that verse is verse and prose is prose—and there it ends. Or, to be charitable, that the proof of the pudding is in the eating; if we turn to the file of illustrative materials, we can find rhyme used discreetly and in minute quantities in prose to secure emphasis; and we can find it used rather more liberally for humor; otherwise, the only authors who go in for the bastard mix are a group of drivel-writers who offer a sentimental slop for the edification of the least intelligent readers. Here is an example:

> Through the long day, set out across the plain to win your goal; push forward might and main. The oxcarts of the pioneers were hurled forward, their hopeful banners all unfurled in the dark night of sorrow and despair, but in the end they found a land to share.
>
> And every hour let there be hills ahead, to challenge our courage and make us lift our eyes to gain fresh faith in future paradise. And as we go, our purpose far ahead, should be to follow in the footsteps of the dead.
>
> *Thoughts for a Confused Day*

The logic of this piece would make a schoolboy's holiday. One hardly "hurls" oxcarts on their way, and banners are not usually unfurled at night. The author's desire for hills would not be shared by most oxcart travellers, nor is it easy to follow footsteps with uplifted eyes, The whole thing, of course, is nonsense.

The upshot is that both rhyme and alliteration have mnemonic and emphasis value, that they are pleasant to the ear when used with restraint; but the man who has no music in his soul should avoid one or the other as a cat avoids water. And wholesale bastard prose-rhyme is mere anathema.

B. ONOMATOPOEIA AND EUPHONY

> "I'll speak in a monstrous little voice,
> 'Thisne! Thisne! Ah, Pyramus, my lover
> dear! Thy Thisby dear, and lady dear!"
>
> *A Midsummer Night's Dream*

A page of print has little more meaning than a sheet of music. Like music, print needs sound to bring out its significance; it comes to life in the voice. It is true that a great deal of our literature is now written for the eye alone, but even in work dedicated to the eye, full values are found only when we also actually hear or listen with a quiet inner hearing. Writing, in short, might be called a second remove from reality, for it consists in setting down symbols of symbols, letters that stand for sounds that stand for things.

It is natural that words should be created in a deliberate or unconscious imitation of the sounds of the world; it is inherent in our selves, this imitativeness. A little child is not content to call a cow, a cow; it is a moo-cow, and a dog is a bow-wow; but if onomatopoesy is a child-like quality, then our language itself is the kingdom of children. Such words as buzz, cuckoo, murmuring, thunder, reverberation, whispering, and countless others are primarily imitative of the sounds of the things they symbolize. Of this quality in language poetry naturally takes full advantage—and so does prose.

Tennyson has pointed out what he calls a good piece of onomatopoeia in Milton's *Paradise Lost:*

Thus saying, from her side the fatal key,
Sad instrument of all our woe, she took;
And toward the gate rolling her bestial train,
Forthwith the huge portcullis high up drew,
Which but herself not all the Stygian powers
Could once have mov'd: then in the keyhole turns
Th' intricate wards, and every bolt and bar,
Of massy iron or solid rock with ease
Unfastens: on a sudden open fly
With impetuous recoil and jarring sound
Th'infernal doors, and on their hinges grate
Harsh thunder, that the lowest bottom shook
Of Erebus.

Book II, 871 ff.

This evidence of Tennyson's awareness of onomatopoetic effects was hardly necessary, however, to any reader of his work. Everyone must have noticed the varying sound values of "The Lady of Shalott." One can hear the hoofs of Lancelot's steed and the clash of his armor, one can hear the breeze in the poplars, and there is in the complete poem a pull as of the tide of water rolling irresistibly down to Camelot. The poem might be quoted in full, but here are just two stanzas:

His broad clear brow in sunlight glowed;
On burnished hooves his war-horse trode;
From underneath his helmet flowed
His coal-black curls as on he rode,
  As he rode down to Camelot.

From the bank and from the river
He flashed into the crystal mirror,
"Tirra lirra," by the river
   Sang Sir Lancelot.

In the stormy east wind straining,
The pale yellow woods were waning,
The broad stream in his banks complaining,
Heavily the low sky raining
   Over towered Camelot;
Down she came and found a boat
Beneath a willow left afloat,
And round about the prow she wrote,
   The Lady of Shalott.

The broad open vowels of the first stanza and the minor key of the second, achieved by means of *i* and hard *a*, with the emphasis in both cases of rhyme, leave no doubt of the value of onomatopoeia for many poetic effects.

In the second line of the first stanza Tennyson uses the word "hooves." In Tennyson's time, as in ours, "hooves" was a permissible plural, but "hoofs" was more regular—and Tennyson uses the latter form elsewhere. Why does he use "hooves" in this line?

Onomatopoeia, then, is part and parcel with the world's best-loved poetry from "This is the forest primeval. The murmuring pines and the hemlocks" to "Roll on, thou deep and dark blue Ocean, roll!" Edgar Allan Poe's "The Bells", like hundreds of other poems, and like many and many a piece of the world's music, is nothing but onomatopoeia. And the game goes on, in modern poetry as in ancient, the constant attempt to bring into verse the very sounds of the world about us. A modern poet, James Elroy Flecker, tried to do in his "Brumana" just what Longfellow did in the opening lines of "Evangeline." His poem is worth looking up. D. H. Lawrence played with the vibrations of a piano in one poem, and frequently uses jarring staccato to represent the vulgarity of the world about him. In Keats's "Eve of St. Agnes" we find the words echoing the sounds of a dawn escape:

They glide, like phantoms, into the wide hall;
Like phantoms, to the iron porch, they glide;
Where lay the Porter, in uneasy sprawl,
With a huge empty flagon by his side:
The wakeful bloodhound rose, and shook his hide,
But his sagacious eye an inmate owns:

By one, and one, the bolts full easy slide:—
The chains lie silent on the footworn stones:—
The key turns, and the door upon its hinges groans.

Byron, too, could be the master of onomatopoeia:

Did ye not hear it?--No, 'twas but the wind
Or the car rattling o'er the stony streets;
On with the dance! let joy be unconfined;
No sleep till morn, when Youth and Pleasure meet
To chase the glowing hours with flying feet—
But hark!—that heavy sound breaks in once more,
As if the clouds its echo would repeat;
And nearer, nearer, deadlier than before!
Arm! Arm! it is—it is—the cannon's opening roar!

Childe Harold's Pilgrimage, III xxii

Here is a stanza from the second part of Coleridge's *Rime of the Ancient Mariner:*

Down dropt the breeze, the sails dropt down,
'Twas sad as sad could be;
And we did speak only to break
The silence of the sea.

In this, as in other respects, the whole poem merits careful study.

Without attempting to bring in the whole world of poetry, or even to pause with music, it may be pointed out that one very important element of onomatopoeia is alliteration. In Flecker's "Brumana" the various *s*'s contribute effectively to the susurration of the pines. Similarly in the other pieces, alliteration yields up its share in the total effect.

In prose, onomatopoeia is equally effective. Kipling's liveliest prose is full of it, as is his verse. And here is a remarkable piece from Kingsley's *Westward Ho* that will repay study:

Lancelot sat and tried to catch perch, but Tregarva's words haunted him. He lighted his cigar, and tried to think deeply over the matter, but he had got into the wrong place for thinking. All his thoughts, all his sympathies, were drowned in the rush and whirl of the water. . . . He tried to think, but the river would not let him, It thundered and spouted out behind him from the hatches, and leapt madly past him, and caught his eyes in spite of him, and swept them away down its dancing waves, and then let them go again to sweep them down again and again, till his brain felt a delicious dizziness from the everlasting rush and the everlasting roar. And then below, how it spread and writhed and whirled into transparent fans, hissing and twining snakes, polished glass wreaths, huge crystal bells, which boiled up from the bottom, and dived again beneath long threads of creamy foam, and swung around posts and roots, and rushed blackening under dark weed-fringed boughs, and gnawed at the marly banks, and shook the ever-restless bulrushes, till it was swept away and down over the white pebbles and olive weeds, in one broad, rippling sheet of molten silver, towards the distant sea. Downwards it fleeted ever, and bore his thoughts floating on its oily stream; and the great trout with their yellow sides and peacock backs lunged among the eddies, and the silver grayling dimpled and wandered upon the shallows, and the May-flies flickered and rustled round him like water fairies, with their green gauzy wings; the coot clanked musically among the reeds; the frogs hummed their ceaseless vesper monotone; the king-fisher darted from his hole in the bank like a blue spark of electric light; the swallows' bills snapped as they twined and hawked above the pool; the swifts' wings whirred like musket balls, as they rushed screaming past his head; and ever the river fleeted by, bearing his eyes away down the current, till the wild eddies began to glow with crimson and the setting sun.

Let me hasten to take away the dizzying effect of Kingsley with this little piece from the beginning of a story by a student in my class in creative writing:

Mary Grey awoke with the dust gritting in her mouth and the sound still in her ears, the same persistent whining, humming sound that had always been there through five arid years of wind and drifting earth. She propped herself on one elbow and looked through the window of the sagging farmhouse at the dead vines of scarlet runners that clung to the shreds of broken strings and rustled and swayed disconsolately against the dull dirty grey of the cold October dawn. Dust from the barren farmyard spun briefly in drab spirals, and then subsided into the slow, persistent whispering of sliding sand. The farm buildings beyond the tired rails of a decaying fence leaned wearily before the steady pressure of the wind, their parched boards weathered to a uniform, colorless compromise between earth and sky. The wind droned on monotonously past the corner of the house, while tiny particles of sand sifted through the cracks about the windows and whispered over the worn sill.

For a moment she lay without moving, her eyes dull with the dingy reflection of another day, and then the steady, sibilant sounds slithered through her brain and scratched like finger nails upon glass against the brittle tautness of her nerves.

from "*Ill Wind*"

Now it should be said that no grace of style should be obtrusive. No grace of style should call attention to itself. If it did, it would violate the necessity of economy or chastity. The message is always more important than the manner thereof; and if any particular feature of style obtrudes, it sets a brake upon the smooth communication of thought between writer and reader. The vehicle of meaning slows down or grinds to a stop.

We do not feel distress of this sort when the words are appropriate to the matter, when there is true onomatopoeia or a larger euphony growing out of the meaning. But if the sound becomes more important than the sense, there is a violation of artistic integrity as well as economy betrayed. This is a lesson which Shakespeare learned in his thirties, but which Spenser never learned. It is almost impossible for a complete reader, that is to say a reader who is aware of all the effects whether of meaning or of sound, to read a whole book of *The Faerie Queene* at a sitting without falling asleep. The reason is that in Spenser sound so predominates over meaning that one is lulled asleep by the soothing music of interlinked euphonious interminable stanzas. If Shakespeare had written works as long as *The Faerie Queene* in the manner of his *Venus and Adonis* or *Rape of Lucrece*, he might have had the same effect.

In his early plays, like *Romeo and Juliet*, *As You Like it*, *The Merchant of Venice*, *Richard II*, the cloying, mellifluous quality of the lines frequently defeats their purpose. Here is a passage the world loves—and fails to understand. It is spoken by a sour misanthrope, cynical, disillusioned, and the pictures, once one stops his ears to the music, are every one disagreeable; yet the world lilts through the lines and finds them lovely:

> All the world's a stage,
> And all the men and women merely players:
> They have their exits and their entrances;
> And one man in his time plays many parts,
> His acts being the seven ages. At first the infant,
> Mewling and puking in the nurse's arms.
> And then the whining schoolboy, with his satchel
> And shining morning face, creeping like snail
> Unwillingly to school. And then the lover,
> Sighing like a furnace, with woeful ballad
> Made to his mistress' eyebrow. Then a soldier,
> Full of strange oaths and bearded like the pard,
> Jealous in honor, sudden and quick in quarrel,

Seeking the bubble reputation
Even in the cannon's mouth. And then the justice,
If fair round belly with good capon lin'd,
With eyes severe and beard of formal cut,
Full of wise saws and modern instances;
And so he plays his part. The sixth age shifts
Into the lean and slipper'd pantaloon,
With spectacles on nose and pouch on side,
His youthful hose, well saved, a world too wide
For his shrunk shank; and his big manly voice,
Turning again toward childish treble, pipes
And whistles in his sound. Last scene of all,
That ends this strange eventful history,
In second childishness and mere oblivion,
Sans teeth, sans eyes, sans taste, sans everything.

As You Like It, II, vii, 139 ff

At a later time, Shakespeare learned how to make the sound fit the meaning, and nobody goes about lilting sentimentally such a passage as the following:

Ay, every inch a king!
When I do stare, see how the subject quakes.
I pardon that man's life. What was thy cause?
Adultery?
Thou shalt not die. Die for adultery! No:
The wren goes to 't, and the small gilded fly
Does lecher in my sight.
Let copulation thrive; for Gloucester's bastard son
Was kinder to his father than my daughters
Got 'tween the lawful sheets.
To 't, luxury, pell-mell! for I lack soldiers.
Behold yond simp'ring dame
Whose face between her forks presages snow;
That minces virtue, and does shake the head
To hear of pleasure's name;
The fitchew, nor the soiled horse, goes to 't
With a more riotous appetite.
Down from the waist they are Centaurs,
Though women all above:
But to the girdle do the gods inherit,
Beneath is all the fiend's;
There's hell, there's darkness, there's the sulphurous pit,
Burning, scalding, stench, consumption; fie,
Fie, fie! Pah—pah!
Give me an ounce of civet, good apothecary,
To sweeten my imagination.

King Lear, IV, vi, 109 ff

The true meaning of euphony, then, is that "the wordes mote be cosin to the dede." In this respect Browning is frequently wilfully offensive, as in the famous line, "Irks care the crop-full bird? Frets doubt the maw-crammed beast?" There is no excuse in the meaning for making this line so jolting, so cacophonous; if there were, if the sounds were really appropriate to the message, nobody could object. There is cacophony in the passage quoted from Milton's *Paradise Lost*, but it fits the meaning with exact precision; it is therefore, in the larger sense, euphonious. The passage from *Lear* has many disagreeable sounds; they belong there. But is there any excuse for such everyday echoics as, "The present president," "The old visitor viewed the vista," "They made hay all day," "Not nearly as clearly appearing," or that passage full of *c*'s from Lord Macaulay?

Now it is true that many persons read as though they were deaf. They may be the more blessed in that they shut out a great deal of unpleasantness, but a complete reader is aware of all the qualities of writing. The greatest writers have hearing as sensitive and as acute as that of a composer. Indeed, writers are composers; and we should realize that printed words, like a musical score, come alive when sound is added. Among prose writers, one of those most vitally interested in the sound of writing was Robert Louis Stevenson, whose *Essays in the Art of Writing* (1905) is still worth the attention of any serious student of writing.

Elsewhere in this book I have remarked that style for the sake of style is the vainest of all vanities—and argument for the sake of argument falls under the same curse. This is not to say that we may not get great fun out of exasperating our stodgier neighbors by arguing the hopeless other side. We can get not only fun out of the experience, but increased mental agility and reasoning power. But in serious matters, it is perilous to argue for the sake of arguing; and Stevenson, in his labored analysis of various writing styles, is guilty of riding his hobby too far. If Shakespeare had had to concern himself with PVF's and SLW's, he would never have completed three plays, let alone thirty-six. What we can say—and Stevenson would probably have agreed—is that a writer needs an ear. He needs a sense of color too.

No matter what he writes he needs an ear. Whether it may be a catchy jingle, an epic, a novel, a legal brief, or a sermon, the writer needs an ear. That poetry deals intimately with sound hardly needs statement, but so does prose—and if you don't believe me, just listen to some scientist or professor wrestling in public with a paper on Cancer or Field Mice which he has written mindful of the soundness of his facts, but forgetful of the possible smoothness and beauty of our common speech.

C. SENSE APPEAL

> "My task which I am trying to achieve is, by the power of the written word to make you hear, to make you feel—it is, before all, to make you *see*."
>
> Joseph Conrad

The most skilful teacher in the history of the world was the Christian Church of the Middle Ages. In Normal Schools and schools of Education, teachers in training are taught that an appeal to two senses is more likely to be successful than an appeal to one; and an expert teacher, while he is addressing the ears of his pupils, will be forever sketching on the blackboard and speaking to their eyes. But the Church of the Middle Ages, and to a lesser degree the modern Church, appealed to all five senses!

The appeal to the eyes was made in stained glass and carvings and statuary, in altar screens and chapels and the vestments of the clergy and choir; and wherever symbolism could be worked in, it was worked in. Every piece of the vestments, stole and alb and surplice, had its meaning and its value; and the wandering or inattentive gaze could find nothing that would not speak of the mysteries of our religion. The appeal to the ear came in the magnificent music of the Mass, in those tremendous hyms, like "Dies Irae" and "Te Deum" that have never lost their profound impressiveness—and there were as well the chanting and prayers and sermons. And all these in halls acoustically fitted to render them at their supreme best. The appeal to the touch came in the carvings of pew and pillar, in the very feel of the House of God, and in the hand of the priest resting on the head of the penitent. The appeal to the sense of smell was very strong in the incense, the fragrance of holiness; and in the most moving and meaningful of all ceremonies came the appeal to the sense of taste: "Take, eat, this is My body—drink, this is My blood."

The artist, also, is a teacher; and it is necessary for him, if his teaching is to reach the highest level, to appeal to as many senses as possible. But he is more than a teacher; he is the quickener, the life-giver; it is he who brings to men and women a new sense of the wonder of things and the significance of the word.

> For, don't you mark? We're made so that we love
> First when we see them painted, things we have passed
> Perhaps a hundred times nor cared to see;
> And so they are better, painted—better to us,
> Which is the same thing. Art was given for that;
> God uses us to help each other so,
> Lending our minds out.

The writer who hopes to be an artist must not neglect every appeal to the senses.

But we have already been dealing with this appeal. Alliteration and onomatopoeia are only special forms of the appeal to the ear that is the most readily achieved of appeals for writers. And Rhythm, to be discussed later, appeals to the same sense. Some kinds of Imagery may also appeal to the ear. So, indeed, may some kinds of Suggestion. But we must, as far as possible, appeal to the whole man—and this we cannot do unless we ourselves develop as whole men, with every sense alert. For the saying of the Romans remains true in all ages, that the style is the man, and our shortcomings will be only too evident in what we write.

The chief values in sense appeal will derive, of course, from Significant Detail [See Part II B] and from Imagery [See Part III G] but many details will have no appeal to the senses, and many images will be almost purely intellectual. Nevertheless, if we sought to picture, say, a fire realistically, we should realize that fire is one of the most compelling interests of human beings, and our description should suggest its light and color and warmth and activity—and these details are unlikely to be evocative without imagery:

> The crowd opened up when she got to them, and let her through, and even the cordon of volunteers allowed her to pass. She stopped a few feet from them, her face toward the fire. Against the lurid brightness of the flaming mill, she was silhouetted like a statue in ebony, and as motionless, while the beams of the old building

cracked like gunshots, hurling showers of sparks skyward to mingle with the thick black, writhing smoke. . . . The fire roared with a sound like sudden triumph as the roof of the mill fell, crashing inside the flaming walls, and then as suddenly was almost quiet, as though resting for a final assault. In the midst of that sudden vacuum of sound, Mona Jackson spoke.

The very style here, which is broken, suggests activity and the glare of a major conflagration. This is not to say that the author said to himself, "The best way to convey the impression I wish to is break the rhythm into short, sharp groups, and speak of the flaming brightness of the scene." No; but the author had all his senses at work, and to his mental realization of the scene there sprang words to produce the written picture of what his imagination saw and heard. The appeal in this piece is largely to the eye and ear—and notice, also, the effect of the sudden silence at the end.

In poetry, Keats is among the most sensuous of writers, and a close study of his work is like a course in sense appeal. "Lamia" for example, is in its entirety a manipulation of the reader's full senses, while for a short example of complex sense appeal we might turn to a stanza from the "Ode to a Nightingale":

O for a draught of vintage! that hath been
 Cooled a long age in the deep-delved earth,
Tasting of Flora and the country green,
 Dance, and Provencal song, and sunburnt mirth!
O for a beaker full of the warm South,
 Full of the true, the blushful Hippocrene,
With beaded bubbles winking at the brim,
  And purple-stained mouth:
That I might drink, and leave the world unseen,
 And with thee fade away into the forest dim.

Here is a stanza from Tennyson's "Lotos-Eaters", long a standard example of sense appeal:

There is sweet music here that softer falls
Than petals from blown roses on the grass,
Or night-dews on still waters between walls
Of shadowy granite, in a gleaming pass;
Music that gentlier on the spirit lies,
Than tired eyelids upon tired eyes;
Music that brings sweet sleep down from the
 blissful skies.

Here are cool mosses deep,
And thro' the moss the ivies creep,
And in the stream the long-leaved flowers weep,
And from the craggy ledge the poppy hangs in sleep.

The following piece also makes a strong appeal to the senses:

The Funeral Pyre of Shelley

Three white wands had been stuck in the sand to mark the Poet's grave, but as they were at some distance from each other, we had to cut a trench thirty yards in length, in the line of the sticks, to ascertain the exact spot, and it was nearly an hour before we came upon the grave.

In the meantime Byron and Leigh Hunt arrived in the carriage, attended by soldiers and the Health Officer, as before. The lonely and grand scenery that surrounded us so exactly harmonized with Shelley's genius, that I could imagine his spirit soaring over us. The sea, with the islands of Gorgona, Capraji, and Elba, was before us; old battlemented watch-towers stretched along the coast, backed by the marble-crested Appenines glistening in the sun, picturesque from their diversified outlines, and not a human dwelling in sight. As I thought of the delight Shelly felt in such scenes of loneliness and grandeur whilst living, I felt we were no better than a herd of wolves or a pack of wild dogs, in tearing out his battered and naked body from the pure yellow sand that lay so lightly over it, to drag him back to the light of day; but the dead have no voice, nor had I power to check the sacrilege—the work went on silently in the deep and unresisting sand, not a word was spoken, for the Italians have a touch of sentiment, and their feelings are easily excited into sympathy. Even Byron was silent and thoughtful. We were startled and drawn together by a dull hollow sound that followed the blow of a mattock; the iron had struck a skull, and the body was soon uncovered. Lime had been strewn on it; this, or decomposition, had the effect of staining it of a dark and ghastly indigo colour. Byron asked me to preserve the skull for him; but remembering that he had formerly used one as a drinking-cup, I was determined Shelley's should not be profaned. The limbs did not separate from the trunk, as in the case of Williams' body, so that the corpse was removed entire into the furnace. I had taken the precaution of having more and larger pieces of timber, in consequence of my experience of the day before of the difficulty of consuming a corpse in the open air with our apparatus. After the fire was well kindled, we repeated the ceremony of the previous day; and more wine was poured over Shelley's dead body than he had consumed during his life. This with the oil and salt made the yellow flames glisten and quiver. The heat from the sun and the fire was so intense that the atmosphere was tremulous and wavy. The corpse fell open and the heart was laid bare. The frontal bone of the skull, where it had been struck with the mattock, fell off; and, as the back of the head rested on the red-hot bottom bars of the furnace, the brains literally seethed, bubbled, and boiled as in a cauldron, for a very long time.

Byron could not face this scene; he withdrew to the beach and swam off to the *Bolivar*. Leigh Hunt remained in the carriage. The fire was so fierce as to produce a white heat on the iron, and to reduce its contents to grey ashes. The only portions that were not consumed were some fragments of bones, the jaw, and the skull, but what surprised us all, was that his heart remained entire. In snatching this relic from the fiery furnace, my hand was severely burned; and had anyone seen me do the act, I should have been put into quarantine.

E. J. Trelawny, *Recollections of the Last Days of Byron and Shelley*.

Let me take away the shock of the last piece with a walk in the darkness:

They walked on west again to the bridge over Willow Creek, and then they left the road and followed the path that led along the farther bank. As they left the lights of the town, the night seemed to take on a subtle radiance of its own, and the wind pressed against them warmly and rustled the leaves at their feet. From far ahead a dog barked, the challenge in its voice reduced to absurdity by distance. To the left, a car crawled along the highway, growling at the end of its double leash of light. From somewhere in the town behind them a door slammed, and then the quiet settled about them again more complete than ever. *Vagrant Whistle*

Many of the pieces used elsewhere in this book could have been used to illustrate Sense Appeal; but a wealth of material is available in the work of good writers. Here is a bit from R. L. Stevenson:

It was September, 1429; the weather had fallen sharp; a flighty, piping wind, laden with showers, beat about the township; and the dead leaves ran riot along the streets. Here and there a window was already lighted up; and the noise of men-at-arms, making merry over supper within, came forth in fits and was swallowed up and carried away by the wind. The night fell swiftly; the flag of England, fluttering on the spire-top, grew ever fainter and fainter against the flying clouds, a black speck like a swallow in the tumultuous, leaden chaos of the sky. As the night fell, the wind rose, and began to hoot under archways and roar amid the treetops in the valley below the town. *Sire de Maletroit's Door.*

Finally, we return to Keats, the master of Sense Appeal, and to "The Eve of St. Agnes"; Stanza 30:

> And still she slept in azure-lidded sleep,
> In blanchèd linen, smooth and lavendered,
> While he from forth the closet brought a heap
> Of candied apple, quince, and plum, and gourd;
> And lucent syrops, tinct with cinnamon;
> Manna and dates, in argosy transferred
> From Fez; and spiced dainties, every one,
> From Silken Samarkand to cedared Lebanon.

D. COUNTERPOINT

> "You had that action and counteraction which, in the natural and in the political world, from the reciprocal struggle of discordant powers draws out the harmony of the universe."
>
> Edmund Burke, *Reflections on the Revolution in France*

There is a quality which I have never seen discussed in a textbook or treatment of the art of writing and which I shall call Counterpoint.

Counterpoint in music is defined by Webster as, "The art of composite melody," or "A melody added to a melody, as an accompaniment." It became a matter of serious musical importance in the sixteenth century when it swam into the ken of composers as a technique with philosophical and high artistic implications, but it springs originally from the simple fact that in medieval cathedrals the choir was divided in two parts facing each other across the chancel. This physical division of the choir suggested all sorts of part effects or balanced effects, and multiplied the possibilities of harmony. One half of the choir could sing against the other half, or behind it, as in sixteenth century rounds, and the choir as a whole could escape from the rigidity of unison.

But to say that Counterpoint was a new thing in the world even in the sixteenth century is really absurd. "Is there any thing whereof it may be said, See, this is new? It hath been already of old time which was before us." The forms of art are Protean; they melt and fade and fuse into each other, and the essential idea of Counterpoint is to be found in the strophe, antistrophe, and epode of the Greek dance to which the lyric ode was a vocal accompaniment. And our ballet dancing still is largely contrapuntal in effect.

Now in speaking of literary counterpoint, one must remember the limitation of writing to a sequential order; it is impossible in literature, except as an actual dramatic work may still be called literary, to secure simultaneous effects. It would be quite possible therefore, for a musician to cavil at the use of the word counterpoint here to describe effects not simultaneous but successive. In defence I can only resort to the precedent of Humpty Dumpty, and say, "When *I* use a word, it means just what I choose it to mean—neither more nor less." But if readers prefer to substitute *Interweaving* for Counterpoint wherever the latter appears, I shall not object.

To illustrate the possibility in an elementary or rudimentary counterpoint, the antithetical statement, here is a poem by one of my own students. I must say that this student had never heard of literary counterpoint, and neither the topic nor the technique was given to her; the poem is entirely original. The author is Mrs. W. T. Cutt.

Enterprise Education

"Our book is *Land Across the Sea*—
May I take my wooden shoes to school?"

Land of Rembrandt and Ruysdael,
Land of turning windmills, of red and yellow tulips,
Round red cheeses in the shops, spices from Java,
Jolly skaters on the frozen canals.

Mud, slime,
Water to the waist,
Cattle floating bloated,
Starving people.

Sunny land of grapes and olives,
Raphael's paintings of gentle-eyed Madonnas,
Venice, bride of the sea, and Pisa's Leaning Tower,
Rome where all roads lead.

Winter—mud,
Summer—dust,
Snipers in the vineyards,
Death along the highway.

France: Paris—Chanel and Schiaparelli,
Arc de Triomphe and the Tuileries,
Orleans—the Maid on her white charger,
Liberté, Egalité, Fraternité.

Queues, black market,
Blank, dazed faces,
Lucille, shaven-headed
(Petain au poteau!)

"Our book is *Lands Across the Sea*—
May I take my wooden shoes?"

The quality of the poem is evident at first sight; the poem is an illustration of "the art of composite melody, i.e., of melody not single, but moving attended by one or more related but independent melodies"; it illustrates counterpoint. There are the contrasting pictures, sentimental and realistic, moving through the poem together; and the whole poem forms a criticism of Enterprise Education, an accusation that our children are taught pretty-pretties and not the stark truth. The same contrapuntal effect is evident in the free-running, musical rhythms of the sentimental pictures, and in the jerk by which each time we are brought down to earth in the realistic ones which contain not only shocking details but horrible cacophonies like "floating bloated."

This poem might be dismissed as an obvious trick in developed contrast, nothing more. To make good the claim that counterpoint is a genuine quality of artistic writing, here is an example from Sir Walter Scott:

"Ride your ways," said the gypsy, "ride your ways, Laird of Ellangowan, ride your ways, Godfrey Bertram! This day have ye quenched seven smoking hearths,—see if the fire in your ain parlour burn the blyther for that. Ye have riven the thack off seven cotter-houses,—look if your ain roof-tree stand the faster. Ye may stable your stirks in the shealings at Derncleugh,—see that the hare does not couch on the hearthstane at Ellangowan. Ride your ways, Godfrey Bertram; what do ye glower after our folk for? There's thirty hearts there that wad hae wanted bread ere ye had wanted sunkets, and spent their lifeblood ere ye had scratched your finger.

Yes, there's thirty yonder, from the auld wife of an hundred to the babe that was born last week, that ye have turned out o' their bits o' bields, to sleep with the tod and the blackcock in the mirs! Ride your ways, Ellangowan. Our bairns are hinging at our weary backs: look that your braw cradle at hame be the fairer spread up,—not that I am wishing ill to little Harry, or to the babe that's yet to be born,—God forbid,—and make them kind to the poor—and better folk than their father! And now, ride e'en your ways;—for these are the last words ye'll ever hear Meg Merrilies speak and this the last raise that I'll ever cut in the bonny woods of Ellangowan."

Guy Mannering, Book I, Chapter VIII

It is necessary to point out that there are several strands woven into this texture: Ride your ways; you have persecuted others; you will meet misfortune.

Counterpoint, then, as a genuine quality of good writing, re-enforces what we have said in I B: a paragraph, like a sentence, may be simple, compound, or complex—and so may every unit of writing all the way up to full-length novels, plays, biographies, and treatises. Yet this complexity, or this plurality, need be no violation of unity for the singleness of purpose and idea is equally evident in Mrs. Cutt's "Enterprise Education," in Scott's Meg Merrilies, and in the simple sentence, "Barking dogs don't bite."

The next example of counterpoint is taken from Ruskin:

Turner's "Slave Ship"

The noblest sea that Turner has ever painted, and, if so, the noblest certainly ever painted by man, is that of the "Slave Ship," the chief Academy picture of the Exhibition of 1840.

It is a sunset on the Atlantic after prolonged storm; but the storm is partially lulled, and the torn and streaming rainclouds are moving in scarlet lines to lose themselves in the hollow of the night. The whole surface of the sea included in the picture is divided into two ridges of enormous swell, not high, not local, but a low, broad heaving of the whole ocean, like the lifting of its bosom by deep-drawn breath after the torture of the storm. Between these two ridges, the fire of the sunset falls along the trough of the sea, dyeing it with an awful but glorious light, the intense and lurid splendor which burns like gold and bathes like blood. Along this fiery path and valley, the tossing waves by which the swell of the esa is restlessly divided, lift themselves in dark, indefinite, fantastic forms, each casting a faint and ghastly shadow behind it along the illumined foam. They do not rise everywhere, but three or four together in wild groups, fitfully and furiously, as the under strength of the swell compels or permits them; leaving between them treacherous spaces of level and whirling water, now lighted with green and lamp-like fire, now flashing back the gold of the declining sun, now fearfully dyed from above with the indistinguishable images of the burning clouds, which fall upon them in flakes of crimson and scarlet, and give to the reckless waves the added motion of their own fiery flying. Purple and blue, the lurid shadows of the hollow breakers are cast upon the mist of the night, which gathers cold and low, advancing like the shadow of death upon the guilty ship as it labors amidst the lightning of the sea, its thin masts written upon the sky in lines of blood, girded with condemnation in that fearful hue which signs the sky with horror, and mixes its flaming flood with the sunlight—and cast far along the desolate heave of the sepulchral waves, incarnadines the multitudinous sea.

I believe, if I were reduced to rest Turner's immortality upon any single work, I should choose this. Its daring conception—ideal in the highest sense of the word, is based on the purest truth, and wrought out with the concentrated knowledge of a life; its color is absolutely perfect, not one false or morbid hue in any part or line, and so modulated that every square inch of canvas is a perfect composition; its drawing as accurate as fearless; the ship buoyant, bending, and full of motion; its tones are true, just as they are wonderful; and the whole picture dedicated to the most sublime of subjects and impressions—the power—majesty—and deathfulness of the open, deep, illimitable sea.

The second paragraph here is an example of artistic writing of the finest sort. It should be confessed that the first paragraph has been set off from the second by the present author; and the last is added only for the sake of completeness. Ruskin is running his counterpoint on several motifs here: the sea, the sunset, and the storm. Just run through the paragraph and count the references to the sea, and note their spacing through the paragraph. The other motifs are less dominating, or are subordinated to the sea—unless one may say that the effect of the sky and storm are ever present even when the obvious motif is the sea. There are many other interesting things in this paragraph, but that it is an excellent example of counterpoint cannot be denied.

If counterpoint may be used within a single paragraph, it must be capable of use in larger units of writing. Several examples may be found in Shakespeare. There is not only Mark Antony's speech with its reiterated, "Brutus is an honorable man," and Iago's, "Put money in thy purse," comparable to the poem quoted in this chapter, but the entire structure of *King Lear* is an excellent example of contrapuntal work. The story of Lear and his three daughters is everywhere shown in contrast with the story of Gloucester and his two sons. Lear has two villainous daughters and one good one—Gloucester has a wicked son and a good one. And the play is single in its purpose or point or significance; it is intended to show that there must be better understanding between the elder and younger generations if the whole kingdom is not to crash in ruin. Lear and his three daughters alone could not have accomplished this significance, for in drama, a single instance is not necessarily universal; two of the same, in drama, because of the stringent limitations of the form, take upon themselves far more significance than any two elsewhere; they become a world. And in *Lear* at every point as the two plots run parallel or cross or contrast or interweave—and they are so inextricably interwoven that neither one could stand without the other—they lend strength and point and universality to the play.

It should be said that the element of counterpoint is both difficult to manage and control, and difficult for readers to interpret. For that reason, Shakespeare's *Antony and Cleopatra* has had to suffer the most amazing contradictions of criticism. Here is a sampling:

1. Antony is a man of the most noble and high spirit, capable at times of a thoroughly soldier-like life, and full of kind and generous feelings.
2. Antony is dissolute and voluptuous, and Cleopatra's depravity is congenial to his nature.
3. The passion of Antony for Cleopatra is too obviously spurious to command our sympathy.
4. Antony appears as the soldier and the voluptuary, swayed alternately by love, regret, by ambition, at one moment the great ruler of the divided world, at the next flinging his future away at the dictation of a passionate caprice.
5. Cleopatra is a brilliant antithesis, a compound of contradictions, of all that we most hate with what we most admire.
6. She is this glorious riddle, whose dazzling complexity continually mocks and eludes us.
7. We do not mistake this feeling of Cleopatra towards Antony for love; but he has been for her (who had known Caesar and Pompey) the extreme sensation. She is neither faithful to him nor faithless; in her complex nature, beneath each fold or layer of sincerity lies one of insincerity, and we cannot tell which is the last or innermost.

> . . . At every moment we are necessarily aware of the gross, the mean, the disorderly womanhood in Cleopatra, no less than of the witchery and wonder that excite and charm and subdue. . . . In her death there is something dazzling and splendid, something sensuous, something theatrical, something magnificently coquettish, and nothing stern.

Now the secret of the play is counterpoint. Shakespeare, here, attempted to show us Cleopatra ennobled by her love for Antony. At the beginning of the play she is a vixen, a courtesan, a hoyden, a creature of passion. Even in mid-play she is able to seize a messenger by the hair and drag him up and down her chamber in a paroxysm of rage. But there comes a point when the serpent of the Nile is subdued, and that is the point in the thirteenth scene of the third act when, in answer to Antony's furious accusations, she says in amazement, "Not know me yet?" At the end of the play she is a queen and magnificent, and the words royal and queen chime through the death scene. She is purified and ennobled by her love for Antony.

At the same time, Antony, who enters the play as the "Triple-pillar of the world," is debased by his infatuation for Cleopatra. In the very first scene he contemptuously dismisses messengers from Rome as if state affairs were less important than his pleasures. And at the end he has sunk low indeed, to ignominy, disgrace, and suicide. At the beginning of the play we doubt if Cleopatra is worthy of the greatness, the magnificence of Antony; at the end we know that Antony is unworthy of the "lass unparallel'd."

These lines cross in the play, each constantly setting off the other in unmistakeable light—all that is needed is the clue, and the clue is counterpoint. It is a magnificent performance; and there is nothing in literature to equal the technical perfection, the flawless and brilliant execution of the first scene and the last act of *Antony and Cleopatra*.

Hamlet might be similarly discussed, but this is neither the time nor the place to enter upon a subject so controversial. The point may be stated, even if not proved, that wherever critics become contradictory over great pieces of literary workmanship, the secret of their bewilderment is likely to be counterpoint. And perhaps it should be added that if one really desires to learn to write, he may well give days and nights to Shakespeare who, at least in our tongue, has written best.

Now if counterpoint appears in these plots of Shakespeare, it must appear also in novels and short stories, for it is a matter of historical fact, the idea of plot comes to these prose forms from the drama. It will be necessary here only to mention these forms. But it will be important to insist that to become a good writer, one must develop a many-sided awareness, an awareness of sound and meaning and suggestion. One must not merely learn the values of single or individual stops and keys and pedals that constitute the multitudinous organ of literary communication, but become sensitive to and aware of their values in combination and contrast, in a myriad forms of contrapuntal harmony.

E. SUGGESTION AND TONE

"The light of magic suggestiveness."
Conrad

Don't say it all. Don't try to say it all. You can't say it all anyway, and might as well not try.

Thus emphatically I approach the subject of Suggestion and Tone. It is a common fault among young writers, and unskilful ones, to tell too much. It is better to show, to lay out the evidence and then let readers draw suitable conclusions. Telling requires of readers only a passive receptivity, but showing demands their participation—and it is when readers are full partners in the game that they find any piece of writing most interesting.

Showing is the method of drama. The amazing rapidity of Shakespeare's development as a dramatist may be seen in his handling of the same situation in two plays only eight or ten years apart. In both cases, the audience must know that twins have been separated and are loose in the same town. In *The Comedy of Errors*, Shakespeare makes Aegeon tell the whole story of his life merely to account for this situation. In *Twelfth Night*, Viola asks when we first see her, "What country, friends, is this?" If she does not even know in what country she is, something must have happened—and so we go on picking up clues, learning the situation from what is shown, and becoming partners in the action.

If more is either told or shown than is necessary to the desired inference, the writer defeats himself. Unnecessary information merely insults readers, inspires their resentment. Is it not truly talking down to the reader to say, "Shakespeare, *the great dramatist*,"—or "Robbie Burns, *the Scottish poet*," or "The stars and stripes which *as everyone knows, refers to the flag of the United States*"? The apology *as everyone knows* does not atone for the original offence, but suggests that the reader is nobody. "Tell less than thou knowest," says Lear's fool, the wisest character in the play.

The people in real life whom we call bores are those who insist upon telling it all, down to the last dull, trivial, labored detail, who explain jokes, who consume endless time but never get to the gist of the matter, or who wrap up the core of things in layer after layer of tedious verbiage; but conversationalists whom we love may be full of broken speech, tangential remarks, meaningful silences. They are not pundits, they are not pontifical, they are not schoolmarmish—they refuse to elaborate every last circumstance of how the brown cow died, and we find them bright and stimulating. Among other gifts, they have the art of suggestion.

Now we may get on with our business, and I shall treat in the chapter of Suggestion by Words, Suggestion by Imagery, Suggestion by Detail, Suggestion by Incident, Suggestion by Sound, Suggestion by Literary Echo, and Suggestion by Silence; but as it is unnecessary to tie the chapter down to elaborate, formal classification, I shall try to follow my own sweet will and let the reader hunt for the various types if he cares to do so. And if some of these categories fail to show up, that will be all right too: the reader can go out and find his own examples.

Suggestion and suggestiveness are the same thing, except that suggestiveness is a term frequently reserved, nowadays, for indecent, prurient, or pornographic suggestion.

Suggestion often enables an author to back out of a very difficult situation. John Erskine came up against such a problem in his *Lilith.* He was telling the story of the first man, Adam, and the first women, Eve and Lilith. It was necessary to portray everything as being done for the first time; and Adam and Eve, according to the Biblical story, had two children. Genesis deals with reproduction by means of the metaphor of the tree of forbidden fruit. But Erskine was telling a realistic tale. He presents Adam and Eve as they stand looking over the bars of the cow-pasture gate. The scene becomes somewhat intimate, and the cow gazes in astonishment. That is all. In due time Eve bears a son. The astonished cow, certainly a rare thing in nature, measures Erskine's skill as a writer; but it does save pages of embarrassed and embarrassing writing. This example will illustrate Genung's teaching that, "Some things, after having been prepared for, are better left to suggestion than fully told: such as details that excite horror or disgust, or a particularly obvious event." But if the artistic purpose justifies or demands the use of coarse materials, a frank and unblushing treatment of them is so much more manly and less offensive than that hypocrisy which refuses both to face an issue and leave it alone. It should be added that the art of indecent suggestion is not a difficult one only to be mastered by a few rare persons exceptionally gifted, for the world teems with indecent stories and books.

In a previous chapter we have seen that Ruskin can suggest by the rhythm of writing the very movement of a ship upon the sea. The mere sound of a piece of writing, apart from its meaning, can also express its author's intention. Here is Edgar Allan Poe laying the foundation for a story of melancholy and horror:

> During the whole of a dull, dark, and soundless day in the autumn of the year, when the clouds hung oppressively low in the heavens, I had been passing alone, on horseback, through a singularly dreary tract of country; and at length found myself, as the shades of evening drew on, within view of the melancholy House of Usher. I know not how it was—but, with the first glimpse of the building, a sense of insufferable gloom pervaded my spirit. I say insufferable; for the feeling was unrelieved by any of that half-pleasureable, because poetic, sentiment with which the mind usually receives even the sternest natural images of the desolate or terrible. I looked upon the scene before me—upon the mere house, and the simple landscape features of the domain, upon the bleak walls, upon the vacant eye-like windows, upon a few rank sedges, and upon a few trunks of decayed trees—with an utter depression of soul which I can compare to no earthly sensation more properly than to the after-dream of the reveler upon opium; the bitter lapse into everyday life, the hideous dropping off of the veil. There was an iciness, a sinking, a sickening of the heart, an unredeemed dreariness of thought that no goading of the imagination could torture into aught of the sublime. What was it—I paused to think—what was it that so unnerved me in the contemplation of the House of Usher?

It will be noticed that this paragraph abounds in heavy, dull sounds, in deep vowels and heavy letters like d, p, g, m, and n. The careful selection of detail and image is equally important, and the resulting tone is gloomy. Such is the power of suggestion skilfully handled.

Suggestion and implication, it will be evident, are the same thing. In all our speech and in all our behaviour we are continually making implications whether we are conscious of them or not, just as we are always drawing inferences. Like it or not, in all our writing, the implications are present, and readers will draw inferences. I once heard a most attractive girl say to her friend, "Holy Gee, Mame, was I drunk last night!" Various implications were quite clear, and various inferences might be drawn from that remark. Now I have said several times, and say again, that I don't believe there is any such thing as an unconscious artist; the writer must, if he is to reach excellence, be aware of all that is implied in his work. It is evident that Edgar Allan Poe knew exactly what he was doing—and it is evident that all too often the unskilled writer does not.

The student of the art of subtle suggestion would do well to study the work of Katherine Mansfield—"The Garden Party," perhaps. So the first sentence of that story: "And after all, the weather was ideal," will be found, as the reader goes on, to be full of suggestion of weeks of fretting and preparing and worrying that would take a heavy and possibly dull paragraph. Almost every word in that story is loaded with implications, with suggestions; but in the best work, she is, as all of us seem to be, anticipated by Shakespeare. In sheer perfection of nerve, Lady Macbeth's exclamation when she is told of the murder of Duncan is unrivalled: "What, in our house?"

Women ought to be fascinating writers if suggestion were the whole art of writing, for many of them have a natural gift for that oblique reference which, when it is nasty or cutting, men call cattiness; but it is an extraordinary thing that women usually seem to try to write like men—as if they had cried out to the spirits that tend on mortal thought—"Come, unsex me here; and fill me from the crown to the toe top-full of dull masculinity." It is only rarely that a Mansfield turns up who is content to be what men might despair of imitating, womanly and exquisitely feminine. Here is a student who has the Mansfield touch, Mrs. W. T. Cutt:

"Good heavens, no!" I replied. "Where did you see them?"
"About an hour ago," she said, sitting down heavily and fanning herself with the recipe book.

A man would despair of getting that precision of observation and comment, yet once it has been done its seems as easy as lying. "She" is simply one of those persons who never listens, never answers the question asked, but the one she supposes you might have asked, or the one she expected you to ask. Again, in the same story, "I" becomes somewhat testy:

"Personally, I like her hair!" I objected sharply. I do; it is rather brilliant, but it certainly brightens up a room full of drab blonde and brown heads. "And nobody knows that she's anything but quite respectable. She does her smoking openly at least."
"Your slip's showing, Emily," said Amelia.
"Oh, let it show! I do think you might give Jim credit for knowing his own mind!"

That remark about the slip showing is as good as a page of characterization. Amelia is obviously the person who finds a convenient red herring when she is under attack. One does not need to be told of the dreamy, toneless, inconsequential air with which she makes this remark; nor does one need to be told how much she irritates Emily. By their contrast both characters are revealed.

In *Cavalcade*, Noel Coward shows a group of people rendered solemn, stunned, by Queen Victoria's death. To them it is the end of an epoch, a breach in nature. A small boy says, "Mother, why did Queen Victoria die?" The mother tells him that the Queen was tired and old and did not want to live any longer; and the boy, who has all the while been gazing attentively into her face says, "Mother, may I have another piece of cake?"

In the same picture, two young persons, evidently happy in each other, worshipping each other, are shown going on board ship. The whole incident shouts, "Honeymoon!" There is a quick shift of scene and all that is visible at first is a grey expanse of tossing waves. Then a life-buoy comes closer and into focus, with the name, "S. S. Titanic." This sort of artistry is so easy to achieve that one is inclined to wonder why there is not more of it, but it is said that the producers of the film wanted to make this scene more explicit, to show the whole sinking of the *Titanic* and the young couple, among others, actually drowning. That is, they could not trust the movie audience to put two and two together; they would spell out the meaning for them.

Latin classics are especially strong in their moving power of suggestion. There is perhaps an outside reason. Manuscripts were then written on hides, and hides were expensive. Photographic realism, unselective writing, comes in with cheap paper. Before the modern age it was necessary for the sake of economy to compress the message, and "No word too much" was the fine ideal of writers. Those modern authors in whom the classical influence is predominant are likely to be adept at much in little.

Keats's "Eve of St. Agnes" is, in respect of suggestion, one of the most amazing documents in the English language. Keats permits a girl to undress before our eyes and get into bed naked; he mentions parts of the body that ordinarily stimulate sexual fancies, and he has her lover watching all the while from a closet, yet it is surely impossible to call Porphyro a Peeping Tom, or to think any but the purest thoughts while reading this poem. The whole thing is done by means of continual reference to tapers, angels, windows of stained glass, words which by association lead the mind to holy things; he places us in church were it is impossible to dwell upon indecencies. Other sorts of suggestion in this poem enable Keats to load every rift with ore. This work will repay the closest study: it is rich in texture as a Persian rug; and Ridley's examination of it in the book *Keats's Craftsmanship*, if rather crude in places, at least is able to show that Keats knew perfectly well what a problem he had to solve and how manfully he strove for perfection.

Now it will be evident that Sense Appeal, Significant Detail, Onomatopoeia, Suggestion, and other qualities form, as it were, a literary spectrum, color melting into color, shade indistinguishably into shade, so while we speak of Detail, we may also be discussing Sense Appeal, and when we are dealing with Sense Appeal, we find ourselves in the middle of Suggestion. But green is a different color from purple, however imperceptibly they merge into each other in the rainbow; and Suggestion is a different thing from Sense Appeal. If there were no other difference, Suggestion appeals to the mind, and not to the senses alone.

It is especially so in that type of suggestion which we may call the Literary Echo. We have seen Ruskin in his "Slave Ship" saying, "that fearful hue which signs the sky with horror, and mixes its flaming flood with the sunlight—and, cast far along the desolate heave of the sepulchral waves, incarnadines the multitudinous sea" (Part III, D). What Ruskin does here is to bring into the pattern of his own writing the richness of *Macbeth*, "No, this my hand will rather/The multitudinous seas incarnadine,/Making the green one red." He has brought into his prose the most terrible expression of guilt in the English language, and increased the depth and value of his own writing. After all, he is describing a painting of a slave ship, a ship engaged in one of the wickedest trades known to man. But it is fortunate, or skilful rather, that he does not mention *Macbeth;* if he had done so, we might have felt that he was parading his learning. As it is, if we recognize the phrase, we can have an added sense of pleasure and of intimacy with the author; if we do not recognize it, no harm is done, and the language is still impressive.

Similarly, Carlyle in his "Dante" (See Part II C) speaks of the "known victory which is also death," and sets a chord vibrating in the heart of every Christian.

Perhaps the most skilful of all English writers in adding this lustre to the texture of his own writing through literary echoes is Charles Lamb. Hazlitt is also excellent. Here is an example of the playful spirit of Lamb at work, an example pointed out to me by Dr. R. K. Gordon. Mrs. Battle, in "Mrs. Battle's Opinions on Whist," would have the game more simple and austere than it is and strip the cards of some of their color and pageantry. Against this view, Lamb argues in his person as author in favor of:

"the pretty antic habits, like heralds in a procession—the gay triumph-assuring scarlets—the contrasting deadly-killing sables—the 'hoary majesty of spades'—Pam in all his glory!

"All these might be dispensed with; and with their naked names upon the drab pasteboard, the game might go on very well, pictureless; but the *beauty of cards would be extinguished forever.*"

The origin of the last phrase is to be found in what would seem the most unlikely of all places, yet a place subtly appropriate, Burke's "Reflections on the Revolution in France;"

It is now sixteen or seventeen years since I saw the Queen of France, then the dauphiness, at Versailles; and surely never lighted on this orb, which she hardly seemed to touch, a more delightful

> vision. I saw her just above the horizon, decorating and cheering the elevated sphere she just began to move in—glittering like the morning star, full of life, and splendour, and joy. Oh! what a revolution! and what a heart must I have, to contemplate without emotion that elevation and that fall! Little did I dream when she added titles of veneration to those of enthusiastic, distant, respectful love that she could ever be obliged to carry the sharp antidote against disgrace concealed in that bosom; little did I dream that I should have lived to see such disasters fallen upon her in a nation of gallant men, in a nation of men of honor, and of cavaliers. I thought ten thousand swords must have leaped from their scabbards to avenge even a look that threatened her with insult. But the age of chivalry is gone. That of sophisters, economists, and calculators has succeeded; and the *glory of Europe is extinguished forever.*

One further specimen of this sort may be added. In Thomas Hardy's *Return of the Native*, after Clym Yeobright and Eustacia Vye have met for the first time, there follows this passage:

> They separated, and Eustacia vanished in the increasing shade. She seemed full of many things. Her past was a blank, her life had begun. The effect upon Clym of this meeting, he did not fully discover till some time after.

Hardy points up the exact condition of Eustacia by this reference—and brings into his writing an added value from Browning's "Statue and the Bust"—"The past was a sleep, and her life began." But we may feel that the sentence which follows, "The effect upon Clym, etc." is a little flat after the rich association value of the previous sentences.

Just here a caution may be worth mentioning: before we dare to quote or to echo, we must be sure that the quality of our own writing will not unduly suffer. The diamond should not make the setting look cheap.

These examples will show another value of literary suggestion—it compliments the reader. It says, in effect, "I know you are a well-read, intelligent fellow; I do not have to diagram things for you; you have the education and the wit to pick up the cues." This is a flattery to which readers respond—and surely it is not snobbery but harmless pleasure to recognize an old friend among the quotations or echoes and to learn that someone else esteems him. But as always, we must be governed by good taste. Here is a passage that offended many readers of a modern magazine:

> Angus, having consumed an all-time record of three highballs for one evening, did not feel lifted. For him, the evening had all the flavor of the Last Supper.

It would be hard to match the shocking irreverence and irresponsibility of this remark; yet the author, when taxed with it, was able to point out, while apologizing, that he was president of his church's Board of Trustees. So much for literary echo; but every kind of a suggestion, responsibly used, compliments the reader and pleases him. Indeed, the best way to think of writing, as we have agreed, is that it is a game played between writer and reader. If the reader need not keep his wits about him, his pleasure and his opinion of the author decline together.

Here is a bit from a student's story:

> The other woman, neatly and tidily dressed, looked timidly round at the crowd. She breathed an air of orthodoxy, and seemed out of place in that motley throng. A chronic ailment had left its marks of suffering; her parchment skin had the transparent look seen on those who have been the victims of a long and hopeless disease; her pinched nose and cheeks, and the lines around her eyes, bore mute testimony to the pain she had suffered.

The student is *telling it all*; he leaves nothing for the reader. A simple abbreviation would improve the passage:

> The other woman, neatly and tidily dressed, looked timidly round at the crowd. She seemed out of character in the place. Her parchment skin was dry and transparent, her nose and cheeks seemed pinched, and her eyes were caught in a net of interwoven lines: she was much younger than she seemed.

We must not fail to bring in Shakespeare. Here is the beginning of *Hamlet:*

> BERNARDO: Who's there?
> FRANCISCO: Nay, answer *me*: stand, and unfold yourself!

There you are! Within two lines we know that something is wrong in Denmark. The sentry does not make the challenge; he *is* challenged—what an extraordinary thing! But perhaps Shakespeare knows nothing about military matters; it may be his mistake. Let us go on:

> BERNARDO: Long live the king!
> FRANCISCO: Bernardo?
> BERNARDO: He.
> FRANCISCO: You come most carefully upon your hour.

Something wrong again! In all ages solidiers have cadged time from each other on sentry-go. Either Shakespeare does not know what he is talking about, or there is something unusual in this situation.

BERNARDO: 'Tis now struck twelve; get thee to bed, Francisco.
FRANCISCO: For this relief much thanks. 'Tis bitter cold,
And I am sick at heart.

Still something is wrong: this is no language for men full of strange oaths and bearded like the pard, jealous in honor, sudden and quick in quarrel, seeking the bubble reputation even in the cannon's mouth.

BERNARDO: Have you had a quiet guard?
FRANCISCO: Not a mouse stirring.
BERNARDO: Well, good night.
If you do meet Horatio and Marcellus,
The rivals of my watch, bid them make haste.

Now this is too much! This would curl the hair of any sergeant major or commanding officer—rivals of my watch! A sentry with company! What on earth is going on here?

FRANCISCO: I think I hear them. Stand, ho! Who's there?

Well, at least the right person gives the challenge this time.

HORATIO: Friends to this ground.
MARCELLUS: And liegemen to the Dane.
FRANCISCO: Give you good night.
MARCELLUS: O, farewell, honest soldier;
Who hath relieved you?
FRANCISCO: Bernardo has my place.
Give you good night.
MARCELLUS: Holla! Bernardo!
BERNARDO: Say,
What, is Horatio there?
HORATIO: A piece of him.

Pawky humor! *His* nerves are not on edge. Where have we heard that kind of tepid humor before? He must be a professor. And, as a matter of fact, he is—or, at any rate, a philosopher.

BERNARDO: Welcome, Horatio. Welcome, good Marcellus.
MARCELLUS: What, has this thing appear'd again tonight?

Now we understand. Why? There is the intentional vagueness on Shakespeare's part, which makes it the more horrible, of the word *thing*. When it comes to horror, we must never be too specific, too exact in description, but leave something to the imagination of the reader. In other words, suggest. Notice also the word *again*. The thing has appeared before—and now we know why everything in the scene is wrong: the sentries are all edgy with fear. And we have read just twenty short lines of *Hamlet*, twenty lines which on the stage have the power to grip an audience and chill them to the marrow.

Suggestion is specially useful in matters pathetic or tragic. Too much bleating about sorrowful affairs lessens their poignancy. This is also a principle which Shakespeare well understood, as may be seen when Macduff learns that his wife and children have been murdered by Macbeth. What might we expect of a man who has received such tragic news? Macduff is silent. Malcolm says to him:

> Mericiful heaven!
> What, man, ne'er pull your hat upon your brows;
> Give sorrow words; the grief that does not speak
> Whispers the o'erfraught heart and bids it break.

Suggestion, in short, is allied to Restraint and Understatement, to the good Anglo-Saxon refusal to "emote" that has given us many of the finest passages in our literature.

A somewhat grim example of understatement is the following from Milton. It describes the realm of Chaos through which Satan was to make a long and perilous journey. One episode in that journey gives a perfect picture of what happens in the turbulence of thunderclouds but so far as I know the Air Force does not use it to instruct their pilots in Meterology. But here is Satan looking into Chaos:

> Into this wild Abyss,
> The womb of Nature, and perhaps her grave,
> Of neither sea, nor shore, nor air, nor fire,
> But all these in their pregnant causes mixed
> Confus'dly, and which thus must ever fight,
> Unless the Almighty Maker them ordain
> His dark materials to create more worlds—
> Into this wild Abyss the wary Fiend
> Stood on the brink of Hell and look'd a while
> Pondering his voyage; *for no narrow frith*
> *He had to cross.* *Paradise Lost*, II, 910 ff

The more Milton elaborates upon the vastness and turbulence of this region of chaos and horror, the more powerful becomes that grim understatement. He uses suggestion and understatement over and over again to describe the indescribable: Hell itself, Night, Pandemonium and Chaos.

A chapter might be given to understatement alone. It occurs in *Beowulf* with grisly irony, and it is part of the special idiom of the Anglo-Saxon folk. In passing, an example from the First War. We used to say that it started to rain in France on the fourth of August, 1914, and did not let up for more than four years. I remember trying to groom horses in a place where we were almost knee-deep in mud when the soldier next me stepped out to clean his brush against his curry-comb, with the rain pouring down, and remarked, "Well, they's one thing: they ain't no dust!" Folk virtues, I am convinced, are literary virtues; but let us draw this chapter to a close.

Many things, we must realize, are indescribable. Let someone try to put our Rockies into words, with their unimaginable shapes and myriad flow of quick-changing color! To fly over them is to lose all voice. Can they be so painted in words that a person who never saw them, who never saw mountains of any sort, could visualize them? Who can describe a special sunrise or sunset so that readers will see that one specimen and only that? Or who can picture an armful of flowers? Must I now apologize for dragging in Shakespeare so often? He encountered most of our problems:

> But look, the morn, in russet mantle clad
> Walks o'er the dew of yon high eastward hill.

His answer is that which I have been laboring to enunicate: he does not attempt a complete or a detailed description. He gives us one eastward hill, an impression of coolness, an impression of color, an impression of the gradual coming of day (walks), and lets us fill in the rest, making our own pictures from a few suggestions. An armful of flowers you will find in *A Winter's Tale* at Perdita's sheep-shearing where the magic of a few epithets compels us to picture for ourselves the "bold oxlips", "violets dim", and "pale primroses". Not one of these adjectives is the expected one, not one of them is less than perfect in evocative power.

Now shall we learn this art? Is it, after so many chapters, necessary to answer this foolish question?

F. IRONY

> "Look like the innocent flower,
> But be the serpent under't.
> *Macbeth*

Every student of writing is bound to find Irony a difficult and, indeed, a dangerous grace of style to understand and control. In its highest form it can add vigor and point to the idea expressed, but it can also be cruel and savage, and, as sarcasm, serve as a weapon to injure and destroy. It is for this reason that one shrinks from discussing Irony with immature writers, lest one should foster in them a love of irony for its own sake rather than for what it can do to make an idea clearer and more forceful.

The Oxford Dictionary defines Irony as "A figure cf speech in which the intended meaning is the opposite of that expressed by the words used," and as "A contradictory outcome of events as if in mockery of the promise and fitness of things." Webster says that Irony is "A sort of humor or light sarcasm in which the intended application is the opposite of the literal sense of the words; also, the figure of speech using this." I should not, myself, call Irony a figure of speech, but a quality of writing; but it will not matter much what we call it so long as we can arrive at an understanding of what it is, and how it can be used legitimately and for good purposes.

The word *Irony* meant, in Greek dissimulation; and it was used to describe the affected ignorance of Socrates by means of which he led his pupils toward the truth which was in his mind before he began to question them. The Socratic method is certainly effective for the teacher, but it can make the student feel a fool, and resent what has been done to him, or forget the lesson in a wave of embarrassment. It is for this reason that the writer must be very careful in his use of Irony, for like the scalpel it can kill where its purpose is to heal. In the strictest terms, Irony is always light and gentle; when it becomes heavy and cruel we call it Sarcasm. However, as the two forms differ only in degree, I shall use the term Irony for both.

Although Irony makes no appearance in textbooks of the writer's art, a sizeable literature has been devoted to it. One of the best books on the subject is A. R. Thompson's *The Dry Mock* (University of California Press, 1948). Like most writers on the subject, Thompson confines himself to irony in drama, but he does realize that it may occur elsewhere. Indeed, he finds a sort of archetype of verbal irony in the vulgarism, "Oh yeah," which says yes and means no. He distinguishes three main types of Irony: verbal irony, irony of character, and irony of events. The effect of irony, he maintains, is an emotional discord, a conflict between pain and amusement in the feelings of the audience.

Most of the effective qualities of good writing have their representatives across the tracks; and "Oh yeah" is certainly an excellent example of a crude or elemental irony of words. The same effect, however, can be contrived in the use of even such a word as "yes" or "I beg your pardon" by persons adept in conversational cruelty. Let us say that some papers are missing, and that an irate employer has on the mat an employee supposed responsible. The person blamed says, "I placed those papers on your desk yesterday afternoon at 4:45. You thanked me for them." The employer answers, "Yes?" in a way that reduces the victim to pain and confusion. It is the tone that does it, the tone of contemptuous disbelief—but the single word spoken is itself quite unexceptionable. If the employer had said, "You're a liar!" the other would know what to do—but Irony is the velvet glove and the hidden claw. It is gentle, and cruel. It implies a conscious superiority in the person who uses it, and a conscious desire to hurt; it is precisely the cat that plays with a mouse, with a mouse which, as the cat knows, is helpless, unable to escape or to fight back. Similarly, a woman I knew was chilled to the bone after mistaking a hatless man in a store for a clerk or a floorwalker, when he said, "I beg your pardon." His tone expressed no genuine desire for pardon, since he knew perfectly well that he had committed no offence. Indeed, how could such a person *ever* be offensive! He was affronted at being mistaken for a floorwalker. How could any person with discrimination make such an egregious mistake? He would punish the culprit—but, of course, it was not for him to soil his hands with any such creature as could make such a mistake. Therefore the cold, indignant, "I beg your pardon." What answer could the poor woman make? She could only be flustered and humbled and upset; she could only mumble something vague and get away from him—as he perfectly well knew, and enjoyed knowing.

Now to a certain extent I have myself been writing ironically here in that I speak of this gentleman as superior, but imply that he was only "superior," saying that he could not give offence when I mean that such persons are utterly offensive. And I have been exemplifying what Thompson calls Verbal Irony. In hesitating to discuss Irony, I do so largely out of fear of providing weapons for cruelty.

I shall not follow Thompson's classification, though it is a sound and helpful one; but I shall deal with Irony of Comment (with its extremes of Urbane Irony and the Irony of the Reformer), Irony of Circumstance, and Dramatic Irony. The Irony of Circumstance is really the same thing that Thompson calls the Irony of Events, but it is a broader term which can include mere static facts as well as those developing processes which we call events. It can include also Irony of Character. Irony of Comment seems a better name, more exactly descriptive, than Thompson's Verbal Irony; the term is also broader and more inclusive. Dramatic Irony of the special sort I shall try to illustrate seems neglected in his book.

Irony of Comment

"Oh yeah" is really a comment. It cannot stand by itself, but must have reference to something previously said (or done). To that previous statement (by someone else), it replies with surface agreement and sub-surface disagreement. The effect on the person who is addressed is intended to be painful, to a greater or lesser degree. Further, the value of "Oh yeah" depends upon the speaker's sense of the contrast between the statement he has heard and the actual fact. We might therefore have discussed Irony under Contrast, for it must always grow out of the discrepancies between assertion and truth, between hopes and realization, between appearance and reality, between promise and achievement.

Irony not only springs from this sense of contrast, but it is in itself the handsome devil of speech and writing, presenting a fair outward or overt meaning and a contradictory underlying one. It is the shirt of Nessus, a beautiful garment which poisons and so destroys. The Ironist "leads us down the garden path" with innocent words which in the end develop barbs. In a debate between students from the Oxford Union and the University of Alberta many years ago, concerning the place of Canada in the Commonwealth, a polished wellbred youth from the older world spoke in rebuttal in complimentary and sympathetic terms about his opponents and their anxiety that Canada should be more thickly populated, concluding, "So we learn all that there is *in the minds* of our opponents—the great open spaces!" The debate might as well have closed then and there.

But what of the victims? In a debate, both sides are armed, and those who choose to play the game know the rules. The game is verbal warfare, and everyone knows that there is nothing personal in what is said. However, it is a different thing in real life, and especially if one side is adept at the war of words and the other is not. In this case, irony can be bitter and unfair.

Irony is the deadliest weapon in the whole armoury of writers, and it should not be irresponsibly used. It is like one of those dreadful poisons which disintegrate the nervous system of the victim. A sense of responsibility on the part of the writer is vital. It is as if one said, "If murder is necessary, by all means use irony. Use it against evil, use it against social injustice or wickedness, just as Shylock does:

> Or
> Shall I bend low and in a bondman's key,
> With bated breath and whispering humbleness,
> Say this:
> Fair sir, you spat on me on Wednesday last;
> You spurn'd me such a day; another time
> You called me dog; and for these courtesies
> I'll lend you thus much moneys."

This is powerful irony indeed, and justified by the circumstances. But if irony is to be, not a weapon, but a means of amusement, let the fun be shared by all, by the hearer equally with the speaker.

Another ironic comment of the debater's sort is one attributed ultimately to a Scottish professor, that his opponent "had successfully pursued the hare—indeed, he had brought back some of the tail feathers." After such a comment, nobody can continue the discussion.

Perhaps the best way to realize the force of irony is to have it used upon oneself, or to see it used upon a valued friend. A critic writes about Shakespeare:

> Why Shakespeare was attracted to Anne Hathaway and got her with child three months before their wedding, and whether he married her willingly, we can not know. It may all have been very beautiful. Or it may not.

He need hardly have added the last sentence, unless he distrusted the capacity of his readers—as he probably did. All the values and the implications of irony are there: the conscious superiority and the cruelty of the ironist, his assumption of man-of-the-world urbanity, his apparent innocence, and the poisoned sting. And how can he be answered? He *knows* that the supposed irregularity of Shakespeare's marriage has long since been disproved; therefore the lofty, superior concession, "It may all have been very beautiful." But the confirmed ironist is never content with proof: he must find a contrast between appearance and reality even when there is none. The habit of ironic comment, in short, leads to dishonesty. In the same way, the village joker fed by praise because his early victims "got what was coming to them," becomes an intolerable plague, adding misery to the just and unjust alike.

Even if we find we are not directly involved, it is questionable whether irony of comment does not do the writer himself more harm than good. Does not the ordinary reader feel that there is something specious about irony, as if the facts were distorted for its sake? Irony certainly gives more pleasure to the author than to the reader, and to that extent violates a basic assumption of some importance, that our readers are our guests.

Hitherto we have been dealing with what may be called Urbane Irony, or irony which exists largely for its own sake. However, the Irony of Comment may include a type of irony whose purpose, being far larger than itself, therefore completely justifies it, the Reformer's Irony. Again I would refer the reader to A. R. Thompson's *The Dry Mock*, in which there is a good discussion of the nature of the writer who practises irony. Thompson concludes that the ironist is a sick soul, because he has visions of a better world than he sees around him; whether he is justified in using irony to attack present ills depends on whether he feels there is a chance of improvement, or just amuses himself by lashing an incurable cripple.

I should like to differ with Thompson in that I believe Urbane ironists are the sick souls, but the reforming ironist is wholesome, however savage. Of Swift I should be inclined to say that he was one of the very few souls in his day who were *not* sick. Yet he did fall into insanity before he died. It is always a question of distinguishing and identifying. Many Americans believed that Franklin Roosevelt was insane. Was he—or they? To those who crucified Him, our Lord was a mad man. Was Ibsen sick—or the society he attacked? We tend always to ascribe madness to those who upset or disturb us; to their contemporaries, the reformers are always sick souls at best, and at least often, mad. Even this category is ambivalent, however, for it may be hard to distinguish between the reformer and the fanatic. If the writer is a genuine reformer, I cannot condemn either him or the irony he may employ. It is the Urbane Irony, which exists for nothing outside itself, except casual cruelty, that I frankly dislike, or, as Thompson might suggest, do not understand. The Irony of Comment is like a scalpel: it may be used to maim and disfigure, or it may be used to remove a diseased organ and save the life and health of the body.

It should be recognized that there is very little of urbane irony in our greatest writers. Just here I make a distinction: double entendre, irony, and sarcasm form a spectrum of qualities that melt into each other and become difficult to distinguish. Doubleness of meaning is common to double entendre and irony, as cruelty is common to irony and sarcasm. In double entendre, the doubleness exists largely for its own sake, or for the fun of word-play; in irony the doubleness has a cold and deadly purpose. The distinction between irony and sarcasm may be only a difference of point of view, for the hearer may take as sarcasm what the speaker intends as irony. School teachers are never accused of irony by their pupils, but always of sarcasm; and this accusation the teachers never understand and deny indignantly, failing to realize that what to them is mild teasing or genial fun may have a searing effect upon children. Sarcasm tends to dispense with doubleness of meaning altogether, and to use the bare fang and claw. Or, the distinction between irony and sarcasm may be a difference in temperature: irony is superbly cool, sarcasm is white hot. Irony is as cold-blooded as a snake; but sarcasm is a raging tiger.

For the Reformer's Irony, Swift is of course our best example. Here is a bit from *Gulliver's Travels:*

[The two "mighty powers" of Lilliput and Blefuscu have] been engaged in a most obstinate war for six and thirty moons past. It began upon the following occasion. It is allowed on all hands, that the primitive way of breaking eggs before we eat them, was upon the larger end: but his present Majesty's grandfather, while he was a boy, going to eat an egg, and breaking it according to the ancient practice, happened to cut one of his fingers. Whereupon the Emperor [of Lilliput] his father published an edict, commanding all his subjects, upon great penalties, to break the smaller end of their eggs. The people so highly resented this law, that our histories tell us there have been six rebellions raised on that account; wherein one Emperor lost his life, and another his crown. These civil commotions were constantly fomented by the monarchs of Blefuscu; and when they were quelled, the exiles always fled for refuge to that empire.

Here we are quite obviously led down the garden path; we are induced to enjoy the innocent flower, and are stung by the serpent under it. The death of Charles I and the expulsion of James II, and all the great affairs of France and England during the seventeenth century are seen in new perspective. The irony here is fairly gentle, and it may be wholesome for us. It consists, in essence, in a comment on English history—and it is, of course, unanswerable.

Again, Swift gives us a picture of rope-dancing in Lilliput, and adds:

This diversion is only practised by those persons who are candidates for great employments and high favor at court. They were trained in this art from their youth, and are not always of noble birth, or liberal education. When a great office is vacant either by death or disgrace (which often happens) five or six of those candidates petition the Emperor to entertain his Majesty and the court with a dance on the rope, and whoever jumps the highest without falling succeeds in the office.

In this passage Swift has contrived a very keen comment on politics and office-holding.

In some of his work Swift goes far beyond the gentleness of this satire. A notable example is his "Modest Proposal for Preventing the Children of the Poor People from Being a Burden to their Parents, or the Country, and for Making them Beneficial to the Public." The Proposal is, simply, that the children of Ireland should be used for food. Swift discusses this shocking proposal with the utmost coolness, estimating costs and prices, and discussing the quality of the flesh of children compared with other meats. "I grant," he says, "this food will be somewhat dear, and therefore very proper for landlords, who, as they have already devoured most of the parents, seem to have the best title to the children." And he concludes:

> I profess in the sincerity of my heart that I have not the least personal interest in endeavouring to promote this necessary work, having no other motive than the public good of my country by advancing our trade, providing for infants, relieving the poor, and giving some pleasure to the rich. I have no children by which I can propose to get a single penny, the youngest being nine years old [therefore too tough for food], and my wife past child-bearing.

However shocking this proposal may seem, I cannot believe it proceeded from a sick mind or soul. Rather, the writer must have had one of the few really sane minds and one of the few healthy souls in his time and country. It was the country that was sick and insane, for when we remember the unspeakable poverty and destitution of Ireland in those days, and the horrors engendered by absentee landlordism, we can only say that the persons who did not protest were subhuman.

It is quite true that Swift later went insane, and it may be that the indignation of the latter parts of *Gulliver's Travels*, being more savage, and less ironic than sarcastic—that is to say, more direct and less characterized by double speaking—is an indication of what was to happen to him. In his earlier work Swift could be superbly cool, superbly self-controlled, superbly ironical, and, to say it in a word, there are times in this world when men must fight, and fight to the death: on these occasions we shall be happy indeed to be supported by the icy and deadly rapier of an ironist as sane and wholesome as Swift. But irony for its own sake is a prostitution, just as sentimentality, which is sentiment or feeling for its own sake, is a prostitution.

Dramatic Irony

For Dramatic Irony in general, read A. R. Thompson's *The Dry Mock*, or G. G. Sedgewick's *Of Irony, Especially in Drama* (University of Toronto Press, 1948). These books are excellent. There is an example of what Thompson calls Verbal Irony in a play from which he quotes—*Arsenic and Old Lace* by Joseph Kesselring. All through the play the lines say more than they innocently seem to say. The point is that these sweet old ladies who have already murdered about a dozen persons with poisoned elderberry wine offer a glass to still one more victim. He is so charmed by their kindness that he is eager to sample their hospitality. "You don't see much elderberry wine these days," he says. "I thought I'd had my last glass of it." "Oh, no," says one dear old lady, and the other hands him a glass. "Here it is," she says, and the audience understands that this is, indeed, the last glass of anything he will ever drink. This dramatic verbal irony is close to double entendre in that the words carry a meaning beyond the surface meaning. In drama this further meaning may be hidden even from the speaker, or it may be, as in this case, grimly intended. The entire play is worth study, both for irony and for the extraordinary use of a rather grim plot to produce exceedingly funny comedy.

Another type of dramatic irony is a characteristic of Senecan tragedy. Like the verbal irony mentioned above, it is a fairly obvious device. As such, it appears more frequently in Shakespeare's younger work than in the plays of his maturity. In *Richard III*, Anne curses Richard:

> If ever he have child, abortive be it,
> Prodigious, and untimely brought to light,
> Whose ugly and unnatural aspect
> May fright the hopeful mother at the view;
> And that be heir to his unhappiness!
> If ever he have wife, let her be made
> More miserable by the death of him
> Than I am made by my young lord and thee!

"My young lord" refers to her husband, "thee" to her father-in-law, both murdered by Richard. Anne does not know, while she curses the future wife of Richard, that she is cursing herself, for she marries Richard shortly afterwards.

I shall spend no more words upon Dramatic Irony which is excellently discussed in the books mentioned above (their bibliographies are also helpful), but say only that it is not subject to the strictures which I have made upon Urbane Irony, since it exists for an obvious dramatic purpose.

Irony of Circumstance

In the same way, one need make no apology for exhibiting some examples of the Irony of Circumstance. Of this irony in real life we are all victims frequently enough; it is part of our common lot. A good example in literature is that of Robinson Crusoe, who with high hopes and infinite labor toiled at building a boat which was to end his exile and carry him home. So far, we have the fair promise; and never, surely, could long-enduring and heavy labor have been so willingly and so happily undertaken. But the end contrasts with the promise, for when the job was at long last finished, Crusoe found his boat so huge and heavy that he could not get it near the water. Not long ago our local paper told of a man who had spent his spare time all winter building a boat in his basement. One can well guess his dreams of summer pleasure; but in the spring he found that his boat was too broad and large to go up the stairs and through the door. "The earthly hope men set their hearts upon, Turns ashes." We come home bursting with eagerness to tell the great news, anticipating the pleasure we shall share with others—only to find the house empty. Charlie Chaplin's pictures were full of this irony of the golden promise turned to mute despair. One of the favorites of all time is the story of the Biter bit—And it is based on truth. The farmer rigs up a shotgun to go off as soon as anyone opens the door of his chicken coop—and so punish the chicken thieves. Then the next morning he is thinking of something else and opens the door himself. And there is the commonplace of life and fiction alike of the man who asks his wife, mother, and sister in turn to cut four inches off the bottom of his trouser legs. They all refuse, they all repent—and his trousers are abbreviated by a foot.

Katherine Brush's "Night Club" is an excellent example of this kind of irony. Amy is angry and humiliated because she has caught her husband, Tom, kissing her friend, Sylvia: she confides in another friend, Claire. Amy is consoled by Claire who gives her some worldly advice. Then we have a scene between Claire and the guilty Sylvia—and could expect Claire to issue a strong warning to the culprit. She does, but "because, as you very well know, Tom belongs to *me*." Is it not ironical that the wife, Amy, should receive comfort from the very woman to whom Tom "belongs"? The whole story is worth very careful study, for its whole basis is the irony of circumstance.

"Ill Wind", from which I have already quoted, is another example of a story built upon irony. The wife, after five years of loneliness and poverty on a dried-out prairie farm, finds she can stand it no longer, and takes advantage of her husband's absence in town to leave for the city. An emergency at a neighbor's home checks her flight, and allows her to regain the courage she has lost. She then returns home, full of new hope, to find a note from her husband in which he explains that he is never coming back.

A powerful example of the effect of the irony of circumstance is a short story by Mary Ellen Chase, entitled "Salesmanship." The mediocre salesman has been studying very earnestly a book on the technique of selling, and finds an opportunity to practise what he has learned. He is a little perplexed that a woman should be buying a suit of clothes for a boy whom she has not brought with her, but it never occurs to him that the boy is dead, and what is wanted is a suit for him to be laid out in:

"You said twelve years old? Now, that's an age to keep you guessing, isn't it? I've a boy twelve myself. They're alive to everything at twelve."

So he goes on, trying to establish a cosy familiarity with the customer, just as the book told him to do. And once again, however harrowing it may be, we have to recognize the truth, for "life is like that."

Everywhere in life these ironies exist—and literature, if it is to be at all true to life, cannot neglect them. Oscar Wilde says in his "Ballad of Reading Goal" that "Each man kills the thing he loves." Certainly that was Othello's tragedy. Indeed, we are even told, "Whom the Lord Loveth, He chasteneth"—as the patriarch Job may exemplify. I remember my friend saying, a remark that has ever haunted me, on a day when the world was one complete purity, with silver thaw diamonded on every twig, "You would not believe that there could be anything evil in the world—but there is." Nor can one read far in the literature of the world before learning that in the most beautiful surroundings in the world evil can be found. In his *Tale of Two Cities*, Dickens shows evil in the aristocratic life of France, and numberless authors show the canker in the rose elsewhere. Life is full of ironies, and even ballads have their grim moments:

> O our Scots nobles were richt laith
>   To weet their cork-heiled schoone—
> But lang owre a' the play were playd,
> Their hats they swam aboone.

In the old grace before meat which everyone knows, there are these lines:

> O some hae meat that canna eat,
> And some wad eat that want it.

Our perception of irony in the world, to say it in a word, is the measure of our failure to understand the universe—but here I differ with Thompson who credits the ironist with a "clear vision of things as they are." In my opinion, the ironist has a clear vision of things as they are *on the surface*. To omniscience, nothing would remain ironic.

Or perhaps irony is the measure of our failure to understand as scored against our desire to do so. For surely, if ever man did, Thomas Hardy desired to understand; and we have from him a whole book of *Satires of Circumstance*, not to mention numberless presentations in verse and prose of the ironies of life. Hardy struggles constantly with the ironies he finds plaguing mortals; the student can learn a great deal from a study of his works.

I take Irony of Character to be part of the Irony of Circumstance, The simple cry of bewilderment, "How could you?" is clearly the essence of the irony of character. How *could* you! That is to say, "You are not the sort of person who does such things; we might have expected something better from you."

Many of our most puzzling crimes are committed by persons who could not have committed them. Those sweet old ladies in *Arsenic and Old Lace*—how could they be murderers? Yet we know that they exemplify truth. It is even part of our own lives, this irony, for all of us have done things we could not have done; and our response to these occasions may be mere amazement or that profound and silent astonishment with which we recognize our kinship with evil-doers:—"There, but for the grace of God, go I."

Of the irony of character, drama of course takes full advantage, and so does all fiction. Honest Iago, the man of known integrity, is the devious and unsuspected villain. And Duncan says of Cawdor:

> There's no art
> To find the mind's construction in the face.
> He was a gentleman on whom I built
> An absolute trust.

Then he turns to build a similar trust upon—Macbeth. In *Vanity Fair* the whole character and career of Becky Sharp is one supreme irony, and Aldoux Huxley's Fifth Earl of Gonister, like T. S. Eliot's Prufrock, sufficiently shows that modern writers are equally perceptive of the contradictions or discrepancies of which human character is composed.

"Hence the estate of irony is honorable even though its existence is evidence of the terrible imperfections of human life." It is a sane and wise remark—but I would prefer to say that irony, as we perceive and express it, is evidence of our failure to understand human life and the universe.

Imperfections are not the sole field of ironic vision, nor is our perception of irony limited to human life. Surely the mouse that is caught by the cat and given its brief teasing hopes of freedom is a supreme picture of irony. Surely it is ironic that animals should devour the young they have begotten. It is ironic that the life-giving sun should burn and blight. It is ironic that the rain necessary to vegetation should come in the form of hail that reduces everything to pulp. It is ironic that the structure of the physical universe with stars and suns of appalling and incomprehensible magnitude should be reproduced in the atom. Nor can we say that there are imperfections here: we do not know. The rainbow and the northern lights spread their unimaginable beauty in wastes where no human eye can see them; it seems ironic to us that they should do so, for in our strange human conceit we cannot but feel that all things were made *for us*. This is what Gray implies:

> Full many a gem of purest ray serene
> The dark unfathomed caves of ocean bear;
> Full many a flower is born to blush unseen,
> And waste its sweetness on the desert air.

But suppose these things were not made for us! It is a true saying that to know all is to forgive all. Similarly, because we do not and can not know all, life and the universe teem for us with ironies.

The estate of irony is honorable—only when it subserves some purpose greater than itself; this is true of all writing.

G. IMAGERY

"Now we see through a glass, darkly."
St. Paul

In this book, the term "Imagery" is limited to figures of speech, and to very few of them: Simile, Metaphor, and Symbol. Of these, symbol and symbolism are not commonly regarded as figurative. We may speak of Personification, Hyberbole, and Allegory, but only (*pace* the elder grammarians) as these are types of metaphor. Similarly, Metonymy and Synechdoche are forms of symbolism. Allegory might be excluded were it not, essentially, an extended metaphor, sometimes combined with Personification which is itself a form of metaphor. It will be evident that the figures here included under Imagery all involve comparison. None of them are merely rhetorical, merely grammatical, merely prosodic, or mere deviations from the normal; but they all emphasize the relationship of things.

Simile

A simile is a fragmentary comparison. Falstaff, coming on stage with a diminutive page, says, "I do here walk before thee like a sow that hath overwhelm'd all her litter but one." Shakespeare does not say that Falstaff and his page are like a sow and piglet in all ways. The comparison is only a fragment, a partial one, a shard broken off from what might have been a complete likening of one set of things to another.

Samuel Johnson says, "A simile, to be perfect, must both illustrate and ennoble the subject." Shakespeare's simile is certainly perfect; a more apt or expressive or vivid image, or one that flashes so suddenly and with such telling effect into the mind of the reader, it would be hard to find; but does it ennoble the subject? The word "illustrate" would suggest that the simile is an extraneous thing, an added ornament. Both Webster and OED give the same idea concerning imagery. To Webster it is "used for ornament," and to OED it is, "esp. of an ornate character." To all these authorities, imagery is obviously dispensable, unnecessary. If they are right, then I would reply that imagery cannot be found in the best writing, for the best writing can contain "nothing too much," nothing superfluous. The Falstaff simile can only be considered superfluous in the sense that Falstaff and his page have appeared, and the audience has seen the difference in their size. To the reader, however, the simile is the heart of the matter, and by no means merely ornamental, illustrative, extraneous, or supererogatory.

Burns says in an undramatic piece, and in the first line of it, "My luve is like a red red rose." The simile, again, is a fragmentary comparison. It is neither preceded nor followed by any plain statement or explanation to which it might serve as ornament, illustration, or embellishment. The simile is the thing itself; it is what Burns had to say. We might perhaps argue that there is a statement understood, sunk in the background, e.g., "My love is very beautiful; she is like a red red rose." But if simile is only ornament, illustration, embellishment, or illumination, then Burns has given us the frosting without the cake.

The fact is that if imagery consists in mere illustration or ornament, it should be deleted; it would violate the necessity of Brevity or Economy. Or, to say it otherwise, imagery should be used only for cause, when it is the heart of the matter, or at least germane to it. Beauty has been defined as the purgation of superfluities; if the element be superfluous, no matter how striking or apt it may be in itself, it must be eliminated from good writing.

Here is a sentence from *The Life of Brother Lawrence:* "God's treasure, he says, is like an infinite ocean, yet a little wave of feeling, passing with the moment, contents us." Is it possible to express this meaning as well without imagery?—no other question is pertinent.

To make this matter quite clear, let us suppose that we have as a task the explaining, to people who have never heard of such an idea, what we mean by life after death. Let us suppose that we are surrounded by aborigines of some land that never heard of Christ; what shall be way to them? St. Paul met this problem long ago, and we all know how he solved it:

> But some men will say, How are the dead raised up? and with what body do they come?
> Thou fool, that which thou sowest is not quickened, except it die: and that which thou sowest, thou sowest not that body that shall be, but bare grain, it may chance of wheat, or of some other grain:
> But God giveth it a body as it hath pleased him, and to every seed his own body.
> All flesh is not the same flesh: but there is one kind of flesh of men, another flesh of beasts, another of fishes, and another of birds.
> There are also celestial bodies, and bodies terrestrial: but the glory of the celestial is one, and the glory of the terrestrial is another.
> There is one glory of the sun, and another of the moon, and another glory of the stars: for one star differeth from another in glory.
> So also is the resurrection of the dead. It is sown in corruption; it is raised in incorruption:
> It is sown in dishonour; it is raised in glory: it is sown in weakness; it is raised in power:
> It is sown a natural body; it is raised a spiritual body. There *is* a natural body, and there *is* a spiritual body.

Could St. Paul have made this explanation, or any explanation so effective, without imagery? And is not imagery the bone and sinew and muscle of the thing itself? To remove the imagery is to silence the preacher.

St. Paul may teach us, then, that imagery extends the range of language and of meaning, makes it possible for us to say things that without it we could not say at all. If fragmentary comparison, or comparison of individual qualities of things were impossible, our speech and writing would become itself fragmentary and brutish. If metaphor were removed from language, the Oxford Dictionary could be printed in one volume rather than ten.

Simile may be simple or compound. In *The Tempest*, Prospero says to Caliban

> Thou shalt be pinch'd
> As thick as honeycomb, each pinch more stinging
> Than bees that made 'em.

Here are two qualities, the multiplicity of cells in the honeycomb, and the painfulness of the stings of bees, likened to the pinching Caliban is to receive. It is a sort of two-antlered simile—and the second has the virtue of destroying the distracting notion of sweetness that is dominant in our minds when we think of honeycombs. We may infer that distracting notions must be nullified or avoided. To say that the hair of a beautiful lady is "as black as soot," is to be absurd, for the strongest association with soot is griminess.

An excellent example of compound or multiple simile, comparing his lady not to several qualities of the same thing—as Caliban's pinching is compared—but to several qualities of various things, is the following stanza from Ben Jonson:

> Have you seen but a white lily grow
> Before rude hands have touched it?
> Have you marked but the fall of the snow
> Before the soil hath smutched it?
> Have you felt the wool of the beaver,
> Or swan's down ever?
> Or have smelt o' the bud o' the briar,
> Or the nard in the fire?
> Or have tasted the bag of the bee?
> O so white, O so soft, O so sweet is she.

A special form of expanded simile is sometimes called Homeric, and sometimes Epic. It is simply a sustained or protracted, many-branching comparison. Here is one from Spenser:

> Like as a ship, that through the ocean wide
> By conduct of some star doth make her way,
> Whenas a storm hath dimmed her trusty guide,
> Out of her course doth wander far astray;
> So I, whose star, that wont with her bright ray
> Me to direct, with clouds is overcast,
> Do wander now, in darkness and dismay,
> Through hidden perils round about me placed;

Yet hope I well that, when this storm is past,
My Helice, the lodestar of my life,
Will shine again, and look on me at last,
With lovely light to clear my cloudy grief:
Till then I wander careful, comfortless,
In secret sorrow and sad pensiveness.

Sustained similes and metaphors are often found in sonnets, since the very structure of the sonnet suggests them. Let us look at a Homeric simile from Shakespeare:

Never, Iago. Like to the Pontic Sea
Whose icy current and compulsive course
Ne'er feels retiring ebb, but keeps due on
To the Propontic and the Hellespont;
Even so my bloody thoughts, with violent pace,
Shall ne'er look back, ne'er ebb to humble love,
Till that a capable and wide revenge
Swallow them up.

Othello, III, iii, 453-60

The extended or Homeric simile is felt in modern times to be artificial or rhetorical, and the genius of our age seems out of sympathy with it; it is obviously dispensable, in a narrow or confined sense. Othello could have said, "Never, Iago. My purposes are firm and unshakeable." Nevertheless, similes of this sort can and do build up an overwhelming emphasis and lend richness to the fabric of writing. They damask the cloth.

Metaphor

A metaphor is a telescoped simile; it is a simile which has suffered ellipsis. It is just as fragmentary a comparison as a simile is, but by cutting out the "like" or "as," it achieves an assertion of partial or momentary identity. If Othello had said, "Never, Iago. I *am* the Pontic Sea, etc.," we should have had a metaphor, and in this case a sustained one.

Metaphor is of many sorts. In Personification there is an assertion of identity between a natural object and man. Thus in "A tree that looks to God all day," we have an implied statement that a tree is like a human being—a woman, as we learn later in the poem—who may lift her eyes to heaven in prayer; this statement is telescoped or compressed into a metaphor, and into that special sort of metaphor which involves personification and which is called "pathetic fallacy."

Pathetic Fallacy consists in ascribing human feelings and powers to natural or inanimate objects. A certain amount of pathetic fallacy is inherent in our language itself—evidence of the fact that imagery extends the range of language, increases its possibilities. Thus it is commonplace to speak of rivers that run and brooks that babble, of roaring cataracts and whispering breezes, of the dying year and the pride of spring; but a caution may be added; any element of writing overdone leads to vice, and pathetic fallacy overdone is sentimentality. It is pathetic fallacy, indeed, that leads to the accusation that Dickens is sentimental:

> The day came creeping up, halting and whimpering and shivering, and wrapped in patches of cloud and rags of mist, like a beggar.
>
> *Great Expectations*

By itself, this isolated example might be admired, but when it comes to be a habit, and we get page after page of it, it seems cheap. We should not forget, however, that pathetic fallacy is deeply rooted in our language and has given us many of the most beautiful passages in poetry:

> Gather ye rosebuds while ye may,
> Old Time is still a-flying;
> And this same flower that smiles today,
> Tomorrow will be dying.
>
> Robert Herrick

We have been led into this side track by an impure example of personification. A wealth of pure examples may be found in eighteenth century poetry, and in Shelley's "Adonais" they abound:

> In the death-chamber for a moment Death,
> Shamed by the presence of that living Might,
> Blushed to annihilation, and the breath
> Revisited those lips, and Life's pale light
> Flashed through those limbs, so late her dear delight.
> "Leave me not wild and drear and comfortless,
> As silent lightning leaves the starless night!
> Leave me not!" cried Urania: her distress
> Roused Death; Death rose and smiled, and met her vain caress.

Here Death and Might and Life are all treated as persons who experience shame and delight, who can rise and smile, and caress. So the basic simile, "Death is like a person," is telescoped into the statement that Death *is* a person; this in turn becomes merely an implication residual in the personification when Death acts like a person.

Personification seems to be dying out in our language; it seems to be artificial, mechanical, inimical to the desire for simplicity that underlies modern ideals of good writing. Nevertheless, it does appear frequently, especially in relation to storms and fires:

> At last she managed to turn the handle of her own door and stagger inside; somehow she pushed the door closed again. The wind howled in disappointment and rattled savagely against the window; the snow slid and whispered across the glass.
>
> . . . . .
>
> The fire roared in sudden triumph as the roof of the mill fell crashing inside the flaming walls, and then as suddenly was almost quiet, as though resting for the final assault. . . . Behind her, the flames rose high again, tearing noisily at the dying mill.

Hyperbole is exaggerated metaphor. This statement might make some grammarians wince; but, as we have seen, the whole philosophy of imagery is in need of definition. I reject as hyperbole mere similes in the comparative degree, like: "Swifter than eagles," and "Stronger than lions," and I am unable to think of any real hyperbole that is not built up from a basic metaphor or metaphors:

> For do but stand upon the foaming shore,
> The chidden billow seems to pelt the clouds;
> The wind-shak'd surge, with high and monstrous mane,
> Seems to cast water on the burning Bear
> And quench the guards of th'ever-fixèd pole.
>
> *Othello*
>
> The sky, it seems, would pour down stinking pitch,
> But that the sea, mounting to the' welkin's cheek,
> Dashes the fire out.
>
> *The Tempest*

In that it involves exaggeration, hyperbole is likely to degenerate into bombast, as it does in the hands of many of the Elizabethans.

Symbolism, like simile and metaphor, is a necessary and useful extension of the potentialities of language. The symbol is simply a concrete, readily understood object which may stand for, take the place of, or represent, something less easy to comprehend. When Browning says, "Ah, but a man's reach should exceed his grasp," he has expressed, through the symbols *reach* and *grasp* an idea which could not be so simply, so forcefully, or so intelligibly expressed otherwise. The minds of most human beings are geared to the finite, the concrete, the tangible, a fact which makes the Parables of the New Testament infinitely appealing and instructive. "Behold, a sower went forth to sow"—but the parable does not concern farming; rather it is a dissertation upon the difficulty of inculcating the doctrine of Christianity, of sowing the word of God. It is little wonder that religion, which deals so largely in the abstract, should be compelled to seek out symbols by means of which the faithful may be instructed. But the same need for symbolism is found everywhere. We know that enthusiastic love for one's college or regiment is inspired in anyone through something concrete—"the old red tower," "green and gold,"—or even the football team. To me, Colonel Bogey's March is sacred. It was our march-past music in the First World War. You would see men humping along the endless dusty roads of France, you would see them and feel them and be them, conscious of nothing but one vast ache of the pack that ground you into the earth, of cramped, aching muscles—sweat—chafed crotches—blistered feet. Away up at the head of the line you would hear the first strains of Colonel Bogey, the march for camp for the night, the march-past; little by little the backs would straighten, the feet kick out in a soldier's thrust, as the music got into them, up would come the chins and eyes, the arms would come back to life, the lines would straighten, and the men would swing past the reviewing point at one hundred and forty paces to the minute, stiff as ramrods and proud as grenadiers. This, in a word, is the true value, the meaning of symbolism. It is evident that no writer can afford to be unaware of it.

Indeed, though we tend to think of symbolism only in terms of so great things like patriotism (Maple Leaf, bluenose, Uncle Sam, etc.) and religion (the cross, the babe, Palm Sunday, etc.), it springs from the deepest roots of our being. A friend of mine quarreled with his wife over some trivial matter shortly after their marriage; she tore off her wedding ring and hurled it at him! There it is, a passionate desire for a symbol, for some *thing* concrete to express a large, vague meaning. Perhaps I should mention that they lived happily ever after! It is the commonest of experiences to get into such a stage of vexation and anger that we must smash something—smash some *thing* that represents all the general and un-get-at-able causes of our wrath. It is a commonplace also of criticism that poetic inspiration seeks the concrete, the specific, the tangible, as does any kind of emotion; and the "Song of Deborah" will be a useful study from this point of view:

> I will sing praise to Jehovah, the God of Israel:
> Jehovah, when thou wentest forth out of Seit,
> When thou marchedest out of the field of Edom,
> The earth trembled, the heavens also dropped,
> Yes, the clouds dropped water;
> The mountains quaked at the presence of Jehovah,
> Even yon Sinai, at the presence of Jehovah, the God of Israel.

Faulty Imagery

From what has been said it will be evident that unnecessary imagery, imagery that is stuck on as an added trimming, will not improve a piece of writing. There are also dangers in sustained and elaborated imagery.

Allegory, which is substantially sustained personification, symbolism, and metaphor, has almost disappeared from the world of letters; and few allegories, except Bunyan's *Pilgrim's Progress* and possibly Spenser's *Faerie Queene*, continue to appeal to modern taste. Allegory is felt to be artificial, if not sentimental, and the genius of modern writing demands a tale plainly told. George Orwell's *Animal Farm* a few years ago, a barnyard allegory of the Russian Revolution, in which old Major, the pig, shortly before his death tells of his life and its lessons for the benefit of other animals, has gained popularity; but its chief primary result was the confusion of reviewers.

Even on a much smaller scale than the allegorical, sustained imagery is subject to the accusation of sentimentalism and artificiality. It enforces serious limitations upon an author, also, and it is apt to break down. For example, a student attempting to describe what would be the ideal gentleman of Sir Walter Scott, undertakes to meet the problem in terms of the ingredients of a cake. The ingredients of a cake are flour, butter, sugar, eggs, baking powder, etc.; to speak of magnanimity, courage, and noble birth in such terms is to become rather absurd—and then, there may be qualities that cannot by any stretch of the imagination be forced into the scheme. Moreover, when the sustained metaphor *is* brought off, it will seem to readers to be nothing more than a *tour de force*, and therefore suspect as lacking in sincerity. Further still, only too frequently a sustained metaphor is abandoned because of the difficulties inherent in it—the author tacitly admits failure, admits that he hasn't been able to get the horse across the stream.

If sustained imagery is perilous, mixed imagery is an admission that the writer is not on the job. The student who wrote, "The *hand* of fate has *stepped* into his life and *pricked* that balloon, causing the whole world to crash around him," may have felt inspired, for there is a type of so-called inspiration which is nothing more than self-indulgence, a sort of bath, or bathos, in which one luxuriates while cool reason is lulled asleep. It is for such writers that Dr. Johnson uttered his famous corrective: "I would say to Robertson what an old tutor of a college said to one of his pupils: 'Read over your compositions, and where ever you meet with a passage which you think is particularly fine, strike it out.' "

Mixed imagery has ministered to the fun of the world; but all of us prefer to be laughed with rather than at. Here are some very inspired and unconscious writers:

Step by step and like a rolling snowball, the wily Iago cultivates his seed of suspicion in Othello until he is burning with jealousy.

The efforts of Iago have planted the seed of distrust in Othello's mind, and the growing fear about his wife sprouts a mine of hatred which chokes the tree of good fortune ere he can reap the harvest.

Rosenkrantz and Guildenstern are the King's stool-pigeons sent to ferret out information.

The idea of murder has become the lifeblood of Macbeth and his lady; it surges through their veins like a rising storm.

Jessica also steals her father's jewels and money, a knife-thrust which heaps fuel upon the Jew's smouldering hatred of the Gentiles.

Some interested bystander or some superb private detective will solve the case in hand; and the strong arm of the law is shown up as an idiot.

Often enough, the authors of such gems cannot believe afterwards that they actually studded a paper with them. One lad remarked, "Other people write such things; I don't." All of us, alas, are somebody else! It is somebody else who writes our essays, stories, plays; but our reputation is in the hands of somebody else, and we must watch him with the eyes of a cat stalking a bird.

A distinguished college professor wrote this one: "Penn's melting pot literally bubbled over the rest of North America and fixed the frame of our common social structure." That pot was versatile! Moreover, it did these things *literally*. And, just to set the proper balance, it was a High School girl who wrote of F. D. Roosevelt, "He is a many-sided prism which reflects light charmingly." This is a splendid metaphor exactly used. She meant to say that Roosevelt was essentially shallow, though charming, and that his deeds or ideas should have been credited to others. Now if the man of distinction can err and the child can hit the bull's-eye, the moral is clear: exact and brilliant use of metaphor is not a thing reserved for the greats of the world; it is a power within reach of all of us. Nevertheless, we must be aware of the dangers which beset the thoughtless, the heedless, and the sentimental, for even great men can make asses of themselves, and nothing inspires the distrust of readers more quickly than a false or redundant image. We must always keep control in our writing, leading readers to feel and respond as we wish them to do.

In his excellent little book on *Play-Making*, William Archer utters a special warning against wit-at-all-costs as a disease that plagued English drama for several centuries, and quotes from Sir Arthur Pinero's *The Profligate* a speech by one of the characters who develops the image of wild oats to an extravagant degree, speaking of these wild oats of profligacy thrusting through "the very seams of the floor trodden by the wife whose respect you will have learned to covet!" They even spring up from the chinks of the pavement! He ends by declaring, "And, worst of all, your wife's heart is a granary bursting with the load of shame your profligacy has stored there!" Surely here is imagery gone wild. Archer's text and Pinero's play would be useful to anyone who detects in himself an inclination to allow imagery to take charge of his writing. This is the sort of thing that seems sheer genius in the darkness of the night, but that will not fail to appear ridiculous in the light of day. It might be well to point out also that imagery run riot tends to be the trademark of melodrama in the plays and novels which cannot stand the test of time and are read or presented as farces by later generations.

Somehow, one can hardly believe that wit-at-all-costs can be found in the modern world—but it can. Here is an essay by one of my students:

> To understand what history implies is to envisage a jewel in a setting of rare antiquity.
>
> It is a diamond fashioned in the crucible of time. Treasured in its crystal facets are the ageless intrigues of man who, claiming its table for a stage, performed his petty role. With reasoned care the ancients played their part, and to the brilliant cut added so much of their wit that the modern has not ceased to admire the cullet of their art. The world was old, and man had sung the praises of his dead for centuries before the girdle of his precious gem was realized, and new facets revealed beyond the ken of the ancients. Then vanity set man to "brutage" wherein he failed most miserably, for men may polish, but not shape the evolution of his jewel. Into the crystal is built the essence of all that man proposes. Time detracts nothing from the elixir of truth, but little is added in all the ages of human striving. The gem, itself, is indestructible. Its intrinsic value is gathered from the stream of time from which is garnered only "the first water," the life spirit of great movements. From the eternal flux is saved each infinitesimal portion that adds to spiritual progress, yet in his crypt a king may lie discarded, while the blow of a tyler rings down the centuries.

This essay concludes:

> Vain man! The Present, without history, is superficial; and by the hour, in every breath, is a false mistress—slipping from her suitor's grasp to sleep with History in the silence of eternity, and every moment new history is born. In the end, as he wallows in his bath of mockery, she will return; and then, like vain Marat, the life blood of his endeavor will drain into the catacombs of time, and History will live in his undoing.

One smells Thomas Carlyle here, the worst of models for the modern writer, and especially for a fledgeling. Now there is no doubt that the student spent a great deal of time on this essay, even looking up the whole art of cutting and polishing precious stones; but it was time ill spent. It was time spent in searching out metaphors, in euphuism, in wit at any price—indeed, at the price of the very meaning he wished to express. That meaning is completely lost in the false glitter and false logic of labored metaphors and far-fetched analogies; he is unconcerned about this shocking violation of his own meaning; he is concerned only about *how*, and not at all about *what*. To write so is to prostitute language and to sin against intelligence.

There is also a danger in false analogy. It has often seemed to me that the Biblical image of the Good Shepherd is a doubtful one, even in that most beautiful of Psalms, the twenty-third. A Shepherd raises sheep for slaughter; his care of them is mercenary. But our church Pastors (Pastor is Latin for shepherd) are not mercenary, but interested in our salvation. This image, also, has been hallowed by time; and it may perhaps also re-enforce what has been said earlier in this chapter about the fragmentary nature of the comparison and identification inherent in simile and metaphor.

To recapitulate: imagery is universal in its power and appeal. Its appeal may lie in the fact that imagery is, for the most part, specific and tangible. Philosophers maintain that all knowledge comes to us through the five senses—through extensions of these senses, perhaps, like the telescope and microscope, and through combinations of the gleanings of various senses—but basically and finally always through seeing, hearing, tasting, smelling, feeling. If this principle be true, then we have philosophical reason in their elemental or easily perceptible quality for the universal appeal of simile, symbol, and metaphor; and we may believe Longinus when he says in his essay "On the Sublime", that "The dignity, grandeur, and energy of a style largely depend on a proper employment of images."

Further, imagery springs from the poverty of language. We may indeed have four hundred thousand words in English, but the range of thought still exceeds the range of words; as long as it does so, new imagery will still be necessary, and originality will show, as much as in any other element, in our ability to find the means of expressing those things which words in unfigurative use cannot express.

On the other hand, as new metaphor tends to grow old and settle, ossify, or fossilize in language, it loses value as over-used words lose value; and hackneyed imagery represents nothing but threadbare thought. It should also be remembered that ideas most profound or extensive may often be expressed in the simplest terms, aided by imagery, and that a dissertation graced with a vocabulary broad and varied and recherché, like some vast and complicated algebraic equation, may cancel out in meaning to exactly nothing. Our imagery should suit our purpose, but imagery which has suited old purposes of other men in the past may suit us no better than their cast-off clothing.

Let me conclude with another example. An aged Professor, one who had won his spurs before I was born, and who had a great name in the land when I served my apprenticeship, was pleasant among us at a conference of Professors of English at Oxford in the summer of 1950. He had said, concerning a picture to be taken, and with reference to his great bush of snowy beard, "They should put me in the midst—God the Father, surrounded by a bowery brood of angels." But there was another remark at the end of the conference which I found profoundly moving. He said, "This is the centre! There are no divisions, no provincialisms here, no barriers: it's the centre!" And then he added, "That's what it will be like in Heaven: no Iron Curtain."

Why should the remark be moving? It has its associations, its testimony to a simple, flawless faith; but the real thing is that imagery leaps the barriers, extends the range of language, helps us to understand each other in a flash, directly, clearly, instantaneously, to see, not through a glass darkly, but—as it may be in Heaven or in the millenium—with instant accurate apprehension, face to face.

CONCLUSION

> "Vulgarity is the excess of the means of expression over the content."
> W. B. Yeats

The proverb that the concealment of art is an art in itself has too often been taken to mean that the ways in which artistic effects are achieved should be incapable of detection even by expert critics, and this mistaken meaning has taken in many generations of good writers and critics alike. What the proverb does mean is that the great artist is he who can ensure that his means should not be blatant, that they should not yell or shout, that they should not call attention to themselves at the expense of the whole work of art.

Similarly, we do not call a man well dressed if we can think of nothing in his presence except his clothes. If he is "loud" or fantastic or fancy, he offends our sense of propriety. In selecting clothes, we ask for decency and good material; we do not ask for the raiment that will frighten the children or startle the neighbors. In the same way, if any element in writing grabs attention, jumps out at us from the page, we feel that there is an essential vulgarity in the work. But when we find the writing as a whole pleasing or vivid or effective, we should of course be able to go back and discern the means whereby it became so.

Something more is involved here than the simple question of modesty or vulgarity. It is the principle of Economy.

I must confess to a great doubt concerning this principle of good writing, whether it is the same thing as that Brevity or Chastity which we discussed in Part II, or whether there is a higher level of Brevity, an economy which is necessary to the highest art and should be discussed in Part IV. I shall just spend a word upon it here and leave the question to others.

The immediate phenomenon itself is easy enough to get hold of. Let us say that in drama the playwright must (1) advance the story, (2) characterize, and (3) depict the scene or background. A skilful dramatist does well to advance the story in some speeches, characterize in others, and present the locale in still others; but a Shakespeare can serve all three purposes in a single speech, or even in a single line. This is Economy. "All the perfumes of Arabia will not sweeten this little hand." The line is a necessary part of the action or story. The perfumes of Arabia suggest not women only and their privileges, but a highly restricted group of gentlewomen among whom the crudeness and vulgarities of earthy life are unknown even by whisper; the phrase involves a terrific irony, for Lady Macbeth has fouled her hands with blood! And "little" hand! We have at once an impression of that physical frailty in Lady Macbeth that cannot stand up to the horrible strain she has embraced. We have not even yet listed all the artistic purposes served by this single line, for it echoes in a grim and oblique fashion the earlier great impatience of the same speaker: "A little water clears us of this deed."

So in fiction and in all writing, we are most successful when we oblige our words to carry double and triple burdens—and this economy is impossible if any one element of writing, or any one grace of style, is to shout. When every syllable contributes its share towards the ultimate effect of a piece of writing, and when every syllable is economically burdened, there will be no cheapjack anticking, there will be no individual quality or element calling attention to itself as the surplussage of his costume draws attention to the clown, there will be none of that vulgarity which "is in the excess of the means of expression over the content"—and readers will be tempted to speak of that concealment which, they say, reveals the highest art.

Part IV The Art of Writing

"... burning through the inmost veil of Heaven,
The soul of Adonais, like a star,
Beacons from the abode where the eternal are."
Shelley, *Adonais*

At the end of the long trail our lips fall silent and we prepare for the night. What is there to say? All that has been said in this book was implicit in the Introduction, for to assert that writing consists in the communication of meaning is to say all that there is to say. And it becomes a matter of some weariness to go on drawing out the implications, and the implications of the implications, into the finest, most attenuated threads. And yet the central problem has not even been touched—or, if so, not explicitly: What are the indispensables, the *sine qua non*'s of great art?

Are they matters of technique alone? Browning neatly answers this question. In his "Andrea del Sarto" the faultless painter has come to the bitter realization that he is not an artist at all, but a low-pulsed, forthright craftsman. He looks at a painting by his contemporary, Raphael, and says:

That arm is wrongly put—and there again—
A fault to pardon in the drawing's lines,
Its body, so to speak: its soul is right,
He means right—that, a child may understand.
Still, what an arm! And I could alter it.
But all the play, the insight, and the stretch—
Out of me! Out of me!

The artist, according to Browning, is the man with the insight, the play, and the stretch, who tries to do, and insists upon doing, even better than he can. His technique may be poor, his tools inferior, but compared with the merely faultless workman, he achieves greatness, greatness that even a child may understand. Have we, then, been barking up the wrong tree all this while in presenting a book almost entirely devoted to technique?

Not at all. In artistic workmanship technique is a part, and a large part; but it is not the whole. The faultless painter is not necessarily an artist; and the artist is not necessarily faultless in technique. Art, in a word, is the highest and best expression of meaning; and real meaning badly expressed comes nearer to the ideal than brilliant expression of commonplaces.

This verdict is that of the world itself, one many times expressed. Kipling once rather savagely challenged it when he asked the repeated and cynical question, "It's pretty, but is it Art?" This question he placed in the mouths of the critics whom he wished to attack. He meant to imply that if it is pretty, it *is* art, or perhaps that art does not matter; but his own waning reputation is the answer of several generations. He might, had he always remained at the level of *Kim* and the "Recessional," have received a different answer; but mere prettiness is not art. Neither is propaganda, and flawless technique and brilliant execution are not enough.

On the other hand, here is a man who could hardly speak English and was uneducated even in his own language, Italian, who knew nothing about the techniques of art, and whose last words as he stood sentenced to death are profoundly moving:

> If it had not been for these things, I might have live out my life, talking, talking at street corners to scorning men. I might have die, unmarked, unknown, a failure. Now we are not a failure. This is our career and our triumph. Never in our full life can we hope to do such work for tolerance, for joostice, for man's onderstanding of man, as now we do by an accident. Our words—our lives—our pains—nothing! The taking of our lives—lives of a good shoemaker and a poor fish peddler—all! That last moment belong to us—that agony is our triumph!

But the "arm is wrongly put." Any child could correct it. And, gazing at Vanzetti, the poor fish peddler, in his agony and triumph, we are forced to admit at last that some at least of the indispensables of great art are inherent in the character of the artist. And these, to make a further admission which in the Introduction we indignantly refused, cannot be taught—except as example is the greatest of all teachers. What are these indispensables?

A. SIGNIFICANCE

The first is Significance. If there is no necessary significance in art, then there is no necessary significance in the life of man or in the universe which art represents or comments upon. In all life we insist on meaning; it is hardly strange that we should call for meaning in art. To the littlest child learning to write the simplest things, we insist that sentences must "make sense." We are indignant with grown-ups who do not "talk sense." Why do we insist that every argument shall proceed by reasoned steps from firm premises? Why have we long ago rejected in drama the *deus ex machina*, unless it be that this was a whimsical, capricious, irrational device which did not make sense, which violated our notions of justice? Why do we refuse to accept in drama and fiction the intervention of any accident, unless it be that accident destroys the chain of cause and effect upon which we insist? Even Thomas Hardy, in whose work accident plays a major role, could not have satisfied us had it not been that his philosophy so pervades his work as to make accident a necessary weapon of those grim fates whose playthings his characters are. It is because, philosophically, his characters are *not* the masters of their fates that accident becomes necessary—and therefore meaningful—in his work. But where accident is meaningless, we will not have it.

And now we can resolve a fundamental difference between life and literature. We say that literature must be life-like, but in life all sorts of things happen without apparent cause, while in literature we demand a cause for every effect of importance, and an effect for every cause. If a writer were to present a picture of the random and chaotic appearance of life as we know it from day to day, we are sure to call him insane or foolish. The answer is that whether he realizes it or not, no human being fails to believe in some intelligence and sanity at the heart of things; and our demand that literature be life-like, and at the same time restricted by the chain of causality, is the expression of an implicit faith in the meaningfulness of the universe.

The point is this, that if we walked into some highly complex factory where many operations were going forward at once, we might be bewildered by the apparent chaos; but as we learn how the factory is organized, it becomes reasonable and a model of efficiency. The savage is just as perplexed by the world in which he lives, but the man of science spends his life trying to discover its laws in an unshakable faith that there *are* laws. Modern man may realize that he does not know the meaning of life, but that it has a meaning he does not doubt; and his demand for cause and effect in fiction, in which life is represented, is evidence of his faith.

Or, to say it otherwise, art, like religion and science and philosophy, is one of the answers we make to the ancient command, "Ye shall know the truth, and the truth shall make you free." It is an approach, one of the paths along which we move toward an understanding of the good, the true, and the beautiful. Every artistic endeavor, like every scientific experiment and every philosophic argument, is an act of faith in the existence of an ultimate meaning; and no achievement, whether in letters or in painting or in sculpture or music or any other medium, which fails to contribute, however infinitesimally, toward ultimate understanding, can be called a work of art.

To have done at once with argument, we might challenge anyone to point out an *insignificant* great work of art. There is no such thing.

B.-C. ENTHUSIASM AND RESTRAINT

The second indispensable is not one, but two, the twin principles of Enthusiasm and Restraint.

It is the simple due of the ideas we express, the materials we handle, that they should be set forth with all the attractiveness we can command. If a thing is significant, then that significance must be rendered clearly evident. To act otherwise is to sin against the material. The cabinet-maker with no love for the wood he works with is sure to botch it up; and the teacher who can muster no enthusiasm for his subject is only proving that he ought not to be permitted to teach.

But enthusiasm is not a negative virtue only. Without it, good work cannot be done; with it, we can endure endless strain and hardship and accomplish great things; with it we can secure the audience which our materials demand; for enthusiasm is the most infectious of all things. It catches from man to man; and you will find people interested in the most amazing things only because somewhere behind them some other person was interested. Every university teacher comes to look for students adept in his subject coming from special schools. Here, year after year, are students almost fanatical about physics; they come from School C. Here, year after year, are those equally interested in Latin and the ancient world: they come from School B. Here, year after year, are students keen as mustard over the art of writing: they come from School A—and then, perhaps, no more of these enthusiasts come from School A, and we know that some inspiring teacher has passed to his reward. Or perhaps he has only transferred, and we find coming from School D for the first time our keen young hopefuls.

The lesson of Enthusiasm was one which was learned, perhaps too well, by that great apostle of the Gospel of Work, Thomas Carlyle. One almost calls him Saint Thomas. He says:

> Let a man but speak forth with genuine earnestness the thought, the emotion, the actual condition of his own heart; and other men, so strangely are we all knit together by the tie of sympathy, must and will give heed to him. In culture, in extent of view, we may stand above the speaker, or below him; but in either case, his words, if they are earnest and sincere, will find some response within us; for in spite of all casual varieties in outward rank or inward, as face answers to face, so does the heart of man to man.
>
> *Essay on Burns*

We may quote again the remark made by Moquin-Tandon to Jean Fabre: "If, as I believe, the fever burns in your veins, you will find men to listen to you." The statement is true as sunlight. We may well question whether there is in the world any such thing as a great work of art which has not been accomplished with the aid of burning enthusiasm. To take one example where many might be chosen:

Could Shakespeare have wrought *King Lear* in weariness and boredom? It is a nonsense question. How could it have been done unless hammered out in white heat against the anvil of a man's heart?

But if the law of Significance demands enthusiasm, it also forbids over-doing: the truth must be exact, and Discipline is another name for Art. Unrestrained enthusiasm becomes gush, and gush has not ever spoken as the heart of man speaks to man. From Restraint, moreover, spring some of the finest qualities of art; understatement, suggestion, and that final glory of efficient workmanship, Economy.

Around these focal points of Enthusiasm and Restraint, the art and literature of the world have revolved since the beginning of time. On the one hand there is the Greek temple, on the other the Gothic cathedral; on the one hand there is Bach, on the other Wagner; on the one hand the Classical Age, on the other the Romantic Movement; rococo, and the Venus de Milo; the classical couplet, and free verse; Addison and Swift, and Carlyle and Ruskin; Keats and Whitman, and Wordsworth and A. E. Housman; on the one hand florid exuberance, on the other stark austerity; and the man who fixes his heart upon real greatness must reconcile these extremes, must attain excellence by means of that burning enthusiasm held in by iron restraint which has given us all the masterpieces of the world.

D. SINCERITY

From the Law of Significance we have derived every particle of those technical lessons which are set forth in this book; for it is obvious that comparison and contrast or onomatopoeia or imagery or any other technical aid is only pertinent when we have something to say. But equally implicit in the necessity of significance, and lying beyond mere technique, are the indispensables of great art—and the greatest of these is Sincerity. It cannot be taught.

It can be exemplified. But is it really necessary, first, to show that Sincerity is a requirement that derives from the basic necessity of Significance? To say that a thing must have a meaning is surely to say that the meaning must be clear and uncontaminated, that the author must feel his responsibility toward it, must treat it honestly, must neither add nor detract, must omit the irrelevant or discursive, and say neither more nor less than he means—must, in a word, be sincere. This is what Poe meant when he said that having written the climactic stanza of "The Raven" he would have thrown away stanzas more powerful in effect if he had written any for previous parts of the poem. Stronger stanzas preceding would have caused an anticlimax; and an anticlimax would not have been honest to his intentions and his material. He meant, simply, that without artistic integrity no man can become a great poet. Without artistic integrity no man can become a great writer or a great artist—and one may ask whether a great artist is possible who is not also a great man—but it is possible for a tree partly decayed and rotten to bring forth good fruit.

To every young writer, then, there is presented a clear choice; and the choice must be made. It must be made, and will be made, and may as well be made consciously. On the one hand lies easy fluency, voluminous output—and, quite possibly, wealth as the world counts wealth. On the other hand lies lifelong and iron discipline, infinite pains—and, quite probably, wealth sufficient to one's need. But on this side there also lies character, integrity, sincerity, and the only chance there is of living longer than life.

"In the beginning," says that Disciple whom Jesus loved, "was the Word, and the Word was with God, and the Word was God." I do not know what he meant; but I do know that wherever the word is desecrated, we have degeneracy and death; and wherever the word is cherished, we have the liberation of mankind. A man's word has to be as good as his bond; otherwise there is no point to civilization. And there has to be a time when we "back up" our words, when we say, "On this issue we fight!"

Now Bunyan cannot be called an expert writer. He wrote a great many books, most of which were rubbish. As for skill, in every class of freshmen are students more highly gifted. Indeed, if Bunyan were obliged to write freshman essays on the subjects usually assigned, he would sweat to make his grades. His faults are innumerable, and his vocabulary meagre; freshman instructors would make his life miserable. But on one occasion, he became completely possessed with a theme bigger than himself, and he went after it with absolute honesty and a burning conviction, and became not an expert writer, but a great one. A few of his other works have something of the same quality found in *Pilgrim's Progress*, but it is only in *Pilgrim's Progress* that he does achieve genuine greatness. He is great because he expressed the truth *as he saw it*—and time is the ally of sincerity. So an ill-educated tinker who spent the greater part of his mature life in gaol, author of voluminous trash, he cannot possibly be omitted from any account of English Literature or English History—and we do not see that his greatness is even paradoxical. Why not? Because we all know in our hearts that character and integrity and sincerity are things beyond price in the ordinary commerce of the world.

Shall we learn from Bunyan, then, to despise training? Shall we learn that rhetoric is a disease? Not at all; but we should learn that skill alone and training alone are valueless.

Speaking of "the disease of rhetoric," Ignazio Silone has used the word self-interrogation. It is a word that makes me shiver. In a sense, it is true that Bunyan's greatness, his integrity, is due to constant self-interrogation; but the word suggests a kind of posturing, as if before a mirror, that is one of the other diseases of the world. From it springs a great deal of unhealthy poetry and silly twaddle in general. But Silone's warning is too often ignored. Thus R. G. Collingwood has said in his *Principles of Art* that "Art is the record of a valuable state of mind, and is associated with emotion." Collingwood here is obviously paraphrasing Wordsworth's own "emotion recollected in tranquility," but the notion is an old one, also put rather distastefully in one of Sir Philip Sydney's sonnets: "Fool, look in thy heart and write." How shall I express the corrective?

Sydney does not say, "Look *at* thy heart;" he says, "Look *in* thy heart." Or let me quote an old comment on Shakespeare:

> I have named *impersonality* as his next quality. The term seems strange and rare—the thing is scarcer still: I mean by it that Shakespeare, when writing, thought of nothing but his subject, never of himself. Snatching from an Italian novel, or an ill-translated Plutarch's Lives, the facts of his play, his only question was, Can these dry bones live? How shall I impregnate them with force, and make them fully express the meaning and beauty which they contain? Many writers set to work in a very different style: one in all

his writings wishes to magnify his own powers, and his solitary bravo is heard resounding at the close of every paragraph. Another wishes to imitate another writer—a base ambition, pardonable only in children. A third, scorning slavish imitation, wishes to emulate one school or class of authors. A fourth writes deliberately and professedly *ad captandum vulgus*. A fifth, worn to dregs, is perpetually wishing to imitate his former doings, like a child trying to get yesterday back again. Shakespeare, when writing, thought no more of himself, or other authors, than the sun when shining thinks of Sirius, of the stars composing the Great Bear, or of his own proud array of beams.

This unconsciousness, or impersonality, I have always held to be the highest style of genius.

Rev. George Gilfillan, "Shakespeare—a Lecture."

Hazlitt has made a similar remark about Sir Walter Scott: "This is the great secret of his writings—a perfect indifference to self." The true motto, then, is not "Look in thy heart and write" but "Look at thy subject and write." And write with uncompromising honesty.

This is no new gospel. It is one of the oldest doctrines in the world; as we have seen it, it is the impulse of all art and all philosophy and all science: "Ye shall know the truth, and the truth shall make you free,"—and I make no apology for repeating it. The statement is a categorical imperative, a command, and with the command, a promise. For Truth does not destroy; it liberates—and its other name is Discipline.

But final truth, the ultimate, is beyond us all. Are we therefore shut up to silence? Not at all. We can express the truth *as we see it*, as we understand it, such broken lights as are given to us. The promise will still hold good, seeing that even Bunyan and Shakespeare had only broken lights. Their truths are not complete truths—to us. But it would be difficult to light upon a single work of great art, any work that has lived and been loved by more than a single generation, of which one basic ingredient was not simple honesty.

What does Tchekov mean when he tells us, "A work of art should invariably embody some lofty idea. Only that which is *seriously meant* can ever be beautiful." Again, "And yet another thing: every work of art should have a definite object in view. You should know why you are writing, for if you follow the road of art without a goal before your eyes, you will lose yourself, and your genius will be your ruin." [*The Sea Gull*, Act I]. He means that talent is liberated by truth, that your bread will not rise without the yeast of truth. Until you have something real to say, you will never write well; until you have forgotten yourself in your subject matter, you have never experienced the exhausting joy of artistic achievement. Until you have become as impersonal as Shakespeare, you will not have learned to turn every word, every phrase, every trick in the game, every tool in the workshop to account.

It is not far-fetched, perhaps, to bring in the beautiful story of the woman who went to Buddha seeking surcease from sorrow. Simple indeed was the cure, the easiest thing in the world. "Bring me," he said, "a handful of millet from any house into which sorrow has not entered." The story tells how joyfully she ran to the nearest house, for millet was as common in India as flour is with us. And, receiving the grain, she almost forgot the question, "Has sorrow entered here?" She was obliged to go from house to house, until in the end her own pain was forgotten in the realization of the manifold and multitudinous griefs of the world. No writer who intends his words to endure even as long as the paper on which they are written, can afford to be thinking of himself; he must lose himself in what he has to say. And losing, he will find.

One of the least of the benefits is that self-consciousness at once will disappear from his writing—and conscious art and self-conscious art are as different as day and night. Indeed, self-conscious art is probably a contradiction in terms. And one of the most important benefits will be that such gifts as we have are multiplied more than a hundred fold.

In other words, honesty breathes life into our work. We can be guilty of every fault in the calendar, but so long as honesty may be seen there, we do not speak in vain. This is what both Whitman and Vanzetti teach us, to say nothing of Bunyan. Or, to turn to one of the great documents of the world, Lincoln's Gettysburg Address: we can say only one thing about it, really, and that is that the man did mean what he said. To read it over now, in an entirely different and changed world and with half the context missing, is to understand why there is a monument to this American backwoodsman in London's central roar.

Nor, if our hearts are right, does our work need even to be complete. One of the most beautiful poems in the language, as I've said before, is a fragment, "Khubla Khan." No man can even tell what it means, entirely, for it is only a beginning. And that great edifice of the Middle Ages, Chaucer's *Canterbury Tales*, standing there, with arches uncompleted, empty windows, and whole chapels missing:—surely magnificent nevertheless, one of the greatest documents ever written by man. Chaucer must have known he would never complete his tremendous structure of one hundred and twenty tales and more—he actually wrote hardly a quarter of them—for no man was ever more persistently conscious of the brevity of life. But he cut a supply of quills and took his chance—and after five centuries and a half you may yet hear schoolboys, in bad accent and worse metre, declaiming: "Whan that Aprille with his shoures soote." The fact is, as Stevenson has told us, that "All who have meant good work with their whole hearts, have done good work, although they may die before they have the time they need to sign it."

Now all this preachment will seem sober and solemn, but it need not be. Even humor can be sincere—or it can be cheap and flashy or full of the vanity of self-love, or the other vanity of vulgar appeal. Not a few of our great writers have been, it is true, angry ministers of God; but the greatest of all, like Chaucer, have been sweet-tempered and sunny in disposition, and full of that genuine tolerance for others which we call humor. I therefore close this chapter by reminding you that in an age even more harassing and miserable to live in than this, Dante reserved a special corner in Hell for those who were irritable or gloomy in temper, and who did not smile in the sweet face of heaven.

CONCLUSION

THE DIVINITY OF MAKING

> "For in six days the Lord made heaven and earth, the sea, and all that in them is."
> *Exodus*, 20:11

In the world in which we live, where good is strangely mixed with evil, and the same sun shines upon the just and the unjust, the same food may nourish mean or noble purposes. It seems hardly enough, therefore, to say, like the writers of medieval time, "Go, little book; Demean you fair," and to shrug off further responsibility.

That some sense of responsibility informs this book will be evident to those who have read or studied it faithfully. The emphasis has never been upon the cheap or ephemeral, but always upon the art of writing in its highest attainable forms. It could hardly be otherwise in the work of a teacher, for men who do not believe in the perfectability of human beings will find neither point nor success in academic life: "Their words to wind are scattered, and their mouths are stopped with dust."

But we need not reduce responsibility to the level of immediate or personal practicality, for this question of the perfectability of human beings is tied in also with the general values of education--and surely, in the twentieth century, there is nothing left to us but to believe that the only genuine and dependable hope of mankind rests in constant improvement in the quality and availability of education. We are children let loose in a chamber of horrors, and our only rescue is the attainment of maturity--and speedily.

It is a matter of some moment, then, to plead that this book may not be turned to unworthy purposes. Yet any such plea will be discounted as pedagogical, hypocritical, or priggish. What is one to say?

It is not by accident or whim that the subtitle, *The Way of the Makers*, was chosen; rather, it evolved over the years while this book itself has been in the making. *Maker* was the regular name, during the Middle Ages, for creative writers, and especially for poets. The term poet, indeed (in Greek, poetes), derives from the Greek verb *Poiein* which meant "to make", and the English expression is a strict translation. In the Greek New Testament, St. Paul says that mankind is the poem of God. Of this parallel between artist and God, many medieval writers were deeply, religiously conscious: as God created the earth and all living things, so the artist in his finite realm expresses the divinity of man and imitates the Creator—and so we reach at the end something of that "far broader philosophical meaning" which animated the theory of Imitation held by Aristotle, Plato, and the ancients. Of making, in its true sense, no other animal than man is capable; in making, we approach nearest to that which is divine in us all.

Does it not then seem shameful that we should make for ignoble ends? To do so is expressly to deny that which is God-like in us. It may indeed be that the best a given individual can do, poorly taught as he may be, or the victim of heredity and circumstance, is unworthy of preservation; but surely when a man has gifts and opportunities, there is no horror comparable to that of "making" all his life and still leaving nothing behind. The mind freezes at the thought. The poorest laborer can say, "I dug that ditch," "I planed that board," and the work of his hands will continue for some little time to serve the common good. He can take pride in his effort, and his self-congratulation is earned and deserved. Such a man has enhanced the dignity of the human race and has done his bit to pull us all up from the beast. He is worthy of our Imitation.

If, after so many pages, we come in the end to admit that there is validity in the theory of Imitation, we may look once more at that other theory, of Inspiration, and find some virtue in it also. But the phenomenon, that quickening insight and that heightening of artistic perception, that glow of fruitful pleasure in the work, which we call inspiration, does not derive from any outside source, but from the material itself. It is a sort of happiness unforeseen in the design, which is part of the reward of every sincere and conscientious worker.

Let us say that a man tries to construct a radio cabinet out of apple boxes or plywood. The material itself will split and chip and bend and defeat his efforts. But if the wood is solid and seasoned, maple or walnut or mahogany, he will find the finished work better than his expectations. For when he has planed off the rough and got down to an understanding of the essentials of the stuff in which he labors, he will find a beauty in the grain, an adaptability in the wood that not only lends itself to his purpose but suggests new advantages. These happy touches, this identity of man and material, this integrity of workmanship, this patina of finished artistry, even though not completely understood by an onlooker, communicate themselves to him with something of the same enthusiasm in which the original worker wrought, and he exclaims, "This is inspired!" Inspiration, in short, is the unearned increment of honest effort and good material.

Further, the material we use, since it is not purchased abroad, but derives from our own mind and heart, may minister to our self-respect—or it may not. We may "make" out of scraps and rubbish that lie about on the surface of our minds—and of everyone's mind. Suddenly to say "cat" is to bring the response "dog" from nine persons out of ten. Originality, itself an unearned increment from worthy materials, lies deeper: we must dig for it. And of one thing we may be sure: the workmanship will tend to match the material. To deal in shoddy is to become shoddy.

There was a man who thought he had it in him to write "the great American novel." But for that project he needed time and comfort. Meantime he could write and publish readily enough in a market for which he had contempt. The stages of his deterioration and descent need not be described: everyone knows them. He might have become merely shoddy, but since he really did have an artist's soul and sensitiveness, and since self-respect is as necessary to an artist as air is to the lungs, his end was suicide—and not mere suicide, but a self-revolting wallow of exhibitionism, as if his private self-condemnation were insufficient, but had to be stripped to the quick in public self-torture. "Smooth and easy *is* the road that leads to Hell and destruction."

"Ah, but a man's reach should exceed his grasp—Or what's a heaven for!" The clear choice that lies before us all should not be decided by the criterion of punishment or reward: these are incidentals. In "making" we imitate the divine as we were meant to do; and the inspiration that comes from honest materials and integrity of craftsmanship entitles us to some of that happy surprise with which God looked upon the work of His hands and exclaimed, "That's good!" Every real artist has earned the right to happiness in work that is better than he can do; and every real artist does indeed find the unearned increment.

The way of the true makers, then, is not easy and smooth, but full of thorns and briars and quicksands and pitfalls and perilous rocks; but if we believe in the dignity of man and the perfectability of his expanding universe, this is the only road to take.

BIBLIOGRAPHY

The following bibliography, and the many poems, plays, and stories referred to in the text, together form only a limited glimpse of the material available. The student is reminded that everything he reads is a part of his own experience of the art of writing.

Aristotle: *Poetics*, Loeb Classical Library.

Baugh, Albert C., *History of the English Language*, Appleton-Century, 1935.

Classe, Andre; *The Rhythm of English Prose*, Oxford, 1939.

Cooper, Lane; *Theories of Style*, Macmillan, 1909.

Croll, Morris W.; "The Cadence of English Oratorical Prose," *Studies in Philology*, XVI, 1915, pp. 1-55.

Demetrius; *On Style*, ed. W. Rhys Roberts, Loeb Classical Library.

Elton, Oliver; "English Prose Numbers," *Essays and Studies by Members of the English Association*, Oxford, 1913, IV, 29-54.

Enck, Forter, Whitley; *The Comic in Theory and Practice*, Appleton-Century-Crofts, New York, 1960.

Jespersen, Otto; *Growth and Structure of the English Language*, Appleton & Co., 1923.

Kennedy, A. G.; *A Bibliography of Writing on the English Language*, Yale University Press, 1927.

Leacock, Stephen; *How to Write*, Dodd, Mead and Company.

Marquis, Don; *Hermione*, D. Appleton and Company.

McNight, G. H.; *Modern English in the Making*, Appleton-Century, 1928.

Montague, C. E.; *A Writer's Notes on His Trade*, Macmillan, 1948.

Morton, A. Q.; *Christianity in the Computer Age*, New York, Harper and Row, 1964.

Newsletter, of the American Council of Learned Societies, Vol. XVI, Number 5, May, 1965, pp. 13-24.

Patterson, W. M.; *The Rhythm of Prose*, Macmillan, New York, 1916.

Polletta, Gregory T.; *Intention and Choice: The Character of Prose*, Random House, 1967.

Rickert, Edith; *New Methods for the Study of Literature*, University of Chicago Press, 1927.

Saintsbury, G.; *History of English Prose Rhythm*, 1912.

Sedgewick, G. G.; *Of Irony, Especially in Drama*, University of Toronto Press, 1948.

Shipherd, H. Robinson; *Manual and Models for College Composition.*

Silone, Ignazio; "Rhetoric or Life," translated by Eric Mosbacher, *The Nation*, April 24, 1937.

Sutherland, James; "Some Aspects of Eighteenth Century Prose," in *Essays on the Eighteenth Century*, presented to David Nichol Smith, Oxford: Clarendon, 1945.

Taylor, Warner; "The Prose Style of Samuel Johnson," *University of Wisconsin Studies in Language and Literature*, II, 1918.

Tempest, N. R.; *The Rhythm of English Prose*, Cambridge University Press, 1930.

Thompson, A. R.; *The Dry Mock*, University of California Press, 1948.

Weathers and Winchester; *The Strategy of Style*, McGraw-Hill, New York, 1967.

Western, August; *On Sentence-Rhythm and Word-Order in Modern English*, Christiana, 1908.

Wilson, J. Dover; *What Happens in Hamlet*, Cambridge University Press, 1935.

Wimsatt, W. K.; *The Prose Style of Dr. Johnson*, Yale University Press, 1941.

Yule, G. Udny; *The Statistical Study of Literary Vocabulary*, London, Charles Griffin and Company, 1937.

www.ingramcontent.com/pod-product-compliance
Lightning Source LLC
Chambersburg PA
CBHW031253090426
42742CB00007B/441
9781573832922